PENGUIN CLASSICS

COLLECTED POEMS

PATRICK KAVANAGH was born in Inniskeen, County Monaghan, in 1904. His verse collections included *Ploughman and Other Poems* (1936), *A Soul for Sale* (1947) and *Come Dance with Kitty Stobling and Other Poems* (1960). He also wrote the novel *Tarry Flynn* (1948) and an autobiography, *The Green Fool* (1938). He died in 1967.

ANTOINETTE QUINN is the author of *Patrick Kavanagh: A Biography* (2001) and editor of *Patrick Kavanagh: A Poet's Country, Selected Prose* (2003) and of his *Selected Poems* (1996).

PATRICK KAVANAGH

Collected Poems

Edited by ANTOINETTE QUINN

PENGUIN BOOKS

PENGUIN BOOKS

Penguin Books Ltd, 80 Strand, London WC2R ORL, England
Penguin Group (USA) Inc., 375 Hudson Street, New York, New York 10014, USA
Penguin Group (Canada), 10 Alcorn Avenue, Toronto, Ontario, Canada M4V 3B2
(a division of Pearson Penguin Canada Inc.)
Penguin Ireland, 25 St Stephen's Green, Dublin 2, Ireland
(a division of Penguin Books Ltd)
Penguin Group (Australia), 250 Camberwell Road, Camberwell, Victoria 3124, Australia
(a division of Pearson Australia Group Pty Ltd)
Penguin Books India Pvt Ltd, 11 Community Centre, Panchsheel Park, New Delhi – 110 017, India
Penguin Group (NZ), cnr Airborne and Rosedale Roads, Albany, Auckland 1310, New Zealand
(a division of Pearson New Zealand Ltd)
Penguin Books (South Africa) (Pty) Ltd, 24 Sturdee Avenue, Rosebank 2196, South Africa

Penguin Books Ltd, Registered Offices: 80 Strand, London WC2R ORL, England

www.penguin.com

This collection first published by Allen Lane 2004
Published in Penguin Classics 2005

023

Set by Rowland Phototypesetting Ltd, Bury St Edmunds, Suffolk

Printed and bound in Great Britain by Clays Ltd, Elcograf S.p.A.

ISBN-13: 978–0–14–118693–1

www.greenpenguin.co.uk

Contents

The Poems

1929–38

Contents

Contents

1956–9

Acknowledgements

I first read Patrick Kavanagh's poetry in *Collected Poems* (1964), and wish to record a debt of gratitude and affection to this collection even while superseding it.

I would like to thank the following libraries for giving me access to the poems Patrick Kavanagh published in journals or to his unpublished manuscript poems: the Harry Ransom Humanities Research Center, the University of Texas at Austin; the Mugar Memorial Library, Boston City University; the University of Victoria Library, British Columbia; the Lockwood Memorial Library, State University of New York at Buffalo; the Cambridge University Library; the Morris Library, University of Southern Illinois, Carbondale; the National Library of Ireland, Dublin; the Royal Irish Academy Library, Dublin; Trinity College Dublin Library; the British Library, London.

A special thank you to Ms Norma Jessop, the librarian in charge of Special Collections in the University College Dublin Library at Belfield, which houses the Kavanagh Archive, the largest single collection of Kavanagh material.

James Swift very kindly lent me the typescript of the unpublished 1955 collection.

Patrick Kavanagh's poems are printed by kind permission of the Trustees of the Estate of the late Katherine B. Kavanagh, through the Jonathan Williams Literary Agency.

Introduction

Beginnings

'My beginnings were so peculiarly humble and illiterate
that I have never dared to write about them.'

Patrick Kavanagh,
Poetry Society Bulletin, Spring 1960

The elder son of a cobbler and nine-acre farmer, Patrick Kavanagh
(1904–67) was born and reared in the townland of Mucker in the
parish of Inniskeen, County Monaghan, and left primary school
at the age of thirteen to be apprenticed to his father's trade and to
work the land. For over twenty years he lived the life of the ordinary
young Irish farmer of the period, toiling for a few shillings' pocket
money in fields he expected some day to inherit. (Cobbling increas-
ingly became a sideline as shoe shops and shoe factories opened in
nearby towns, and his parents expanded their farm to twenty-five
acres.) Like other local farmers, he bought and sold at fair and
market, went to Sunday Mass, attended the wakes, funerals and
weddings of neighbours, played pitch and toss at the crossroads,
cycled to dances. He was also goalie for the Inniskeen Gaelic football
team. What set him apart from his fellows was a habit of reading
and writing poetry after hours, usually by candlelight in an upstairs
room, away from the hurly-burly of the family kitchen. Even in his
upstairs hideaway, he was frequently interrupted to perform some
chore. A note on one of his early manuscript collections indicates
the conditions under which these poems were written:

... sitting at the end of the day upstairs in a cold corner by the light of a
candle. A mother's voice calling every now and then, 'Come down and
throw a lock of turnips to the unfortunate cows.'[1]

As the elder son in a family of daughters, he was at his parents' beck and call: 'If it wasn't the turnips, the pigs were after breaking loose, or a hen they wanted me help catch for the fowl dealer.'[2] He seemed destined to outgrow his extraordinary interest in poetry and to end up as 'some mute, inglorious Milton'.

Later, Kavanagh would dispute Thomas Gray's view in 'Elegy written in a Country Churchyard' that a potentially great writer will be silenced by being born into an impoverished underclass living far from the metropolis: '. . . if the potentialities are there, it is almost certain that they will find a way out; they will burst a road,' he said.[3] Yet he never denied the difficulties confronting the self-taught as compared with the university-educated writer who is likely to be put on the right road by 'some strange awakener of genius' in his student days and thus spared a lot of trouble.[4] He was impatient with those who romanticized the under-educated country poet as an inspired lyricist piping down the valleys wild. To Kavanagh, the verses of the self-taught were characterized not by spontaneity and originality but by derivativeness, the imitation of old-fashioned models:

. . . when a country body begins to progress into the world of print he does not write out of his rural innocence – he writes out of Palgrave's *Golden Treasury*.[5]

He was speaking here from personal experience, for he had spent eight years learning his craft from this anthology and from school readers, as well as from even humbler sources, such as the patriotic and emigrant ballads to be found at the back of *Old Moore's Almanac* and in the popular weekly *Ireland's Own*. The influence of these last two models is evident in an early poem beginning

> On the whin-covered slope in fierce battle-array
> Stood the Inniskeen men at the close of the day . . .

Palgrave and the schoolbooks lie behind such lines as

> O break cold heart!
> Thou'rt lost
> For want of wine . . .

and

> I knocked at your door
> And craved one grain of gold
> It would not ope to my knocking . . .

His study of canonical English poetry had convinced the apprentice poet that 'what happen[ed] in his own fields' was not 'stuff for the Muses'[6] and that his vernacular was not a legitimate poetic language.

1929–38

One August day in 1925 while he was at the grass seed market in the town of Dundalk, Kavanagh at last encountered an 'awakener of genius'. Riffling through the magazines in a newsagent's, he came upon the *Irish Statesman*, the weekly journal of arts and ideas edited by George Russell, AE. For the first time he learned of the existence of James Joyce, Gertrude Stein and W. B. Yeats. From then until the periodical folded in 1930, he educated himself from the pages of the *Irish Statesman* and by 1929 was able to produce the kind of vague religio-rural verse of which AE approved. Among the three poems AE accepted was 'Ploughman', printed in 1930 and selected for a London-published anthology of the year's *Best Poems*. 'Ploughman' was to be Kavanagh's passport into literary circles. When he finally plucked up the courage to visit AE in Dublin in December 1931, he made the sixty-mile journey on foot, rather than taking the train, and wore his patched working clothes to impress the ex-editor with his 'ploughman' credentials.

AE was renowned for his encouragement of budding poets, his 'canaries' as Yeats dismissively dubbed them. He loaded Kavanagh with books, lent him back copies of *Poetry* (Chicago) and introduced him to other writers. From then on, Kavanagh often took the train to Dublin to visit AE, extend his literary acquaintance and attend plays at the Abbey Theatre. Seumas O'Sullivan, poet and editor of the quarterly *Dublin Magazine*, took over as his Irish publisher in 1931. This magazine was prestigious and the name Patrick Kavanagh gradually became known in Irish literary circles. Even before he was a regular contributor to the *Dublin Magazine*, his work began appearing in two English journals, the *Spectator* and *John O'London's*.

At the outset Kavanagh was welcomed and patronized as a peasant[7] poet. Peasantry, made fashionable by Literary Revival writers such as Douglas Hyde, J. M. Synge and Lady Gregory, was still a modish literary property in Dublin, abbreviated in Abbey Theatre jargon to 'PQ' (peasant quality). While peasants were frequently encountered on the page and the stage, a farmer turned poet was a literary curiosity. When his first collection was published by Macmillan in their beginners' series, Contemporary Poets, in 1936, predictably the volume was entitled *Ploughman and Other Poems*. It was actually Kavanagh's appearance, gait and south Monaghan accent that proclaimed his small-farm origins. His poetry, though it drew on rural images, could have been produced by someone who had holidayed in the country or was familiar with nature poetry. 'Ploughman', for instance, had come to him while he was tilling an acre of land with a rusty plough pulled by a 'kicking mare'; such inelegant facts as the rust and the unruly mare have been erased from the ensuing poem, where ploughing is transformed into an aesthetic/ecstatic activity. As Kavanagh later observed of the religious poet Philip Francis Little, he was 'all anxiety to read eternal messages in the earthly symbol', not realizing that poetry needs 'a great deal of carnal method'.[8]

Most of the lyrics in his first collection are slight apprentice offerings; their four-line rhymed stanzas, though written in the first person, betray little of the writer's actual context or circumstances. In 'Inniskeen Road: July Evening', however, Kavanagh breaks new ground. The subject, which he treats half-ruefully, half-playfully, is the anomaly of being an Inniskeen poet. This sonnet is allusive rather than derivative, humorously adapting a schoolbook poem (William Cowper's 'Verses Supposed to be Written by Alexander Selkirk') to his own situation. Sonnet decorum is flouted from the outset by the introduction of 'Billy Brennan's barn' and bicycles. The language barrier between the 'half-talk code' of his small-farm class and the 'solemn talk' of the poetic canon, far from intimidating the young poet, is now one of his themes.

In 1936 Kavanagh was still a full-time farmer, hopeful that some rich Dublin patron would pluck him from the fields. When this failed to happen, he decided to try his luck in London, timing his visit to coincide with the coronation of George VI on 12 May 1937. Through the good offices of the Northern Irish poet, translator and novelist Helen Waddell, a reader for Constable, he was commissioned to write an autobiography, *The Green Fool*, and spent the next five months in London working on it. This commission proved a turning point. He was now compelled to describe his own life and small-farm milieu, a subject he had previously skirted or ignored. The very expansiveness of the narrative project – 350 pages of prose – emancipated him from the verbal and syntactical constraints of the minimalist lyric. His autobiography reveals a talent for comedy, an alert ear for dialogue, a direct, uncluttered style, and a capacity to endear himself to the reader by projecting a charming narrative persona.

Kavanagh came to detest *The Green Fool*, condemning it for pandering to the different expectations of two metropolitan audiences: a London readership for whom Irish peasants were comic buffoons with a gift for the gab, and a Dublin literary set who regarded them as nobly primitive, *echt*-Irish figures spouting songs and stories.[9] The book did succeed in appealing to both audiences and was highly praised by reviewers in London and Dublin in 1938 and the following year in New York. Yet Kavanagh's verdict on it was too harsh. While *The Green Fool* undoubtedly sanitizes and simplifies the way of life it describes, it is conscious of literary orthodoxies and often defies them. Inniskeen is not Innisfree.

Unfortunately, Kavanagh's triumphant debut was spoiled when Oliver St John Gogarty took a libel action as a result of an innocuous throwaway remark on page 300 and, to the publisher's surprise, won. It was a dreadful setback for a young writer at the outset of his career and it was not the only disappointment.

A few months previously, Macmillan had rejected a second collection of poems. Kavanagh was by now an overly prolific poet: he still had no sense of direction, was unable to distinguish between the good and the bad among his own verses and asked advice of almost everyone he knew. As 'The Hired Boy' and 'My People' show, he was becoming conscious of his responsibility as a representative of the small-farm and farm-labouring classes. At the same time, his socializing with writers and intellectuals was making him aware of his own educational inadequacies, as he acknowledges in 'The Irony of It'. He was a hit-and-miss writer, occasionally turning out a fine lyric. Seumas O'Sullivan at the *Dublin Magazine* showed critical discernment, selecting three of the best, 'Sanctity', 'Shancoduff' and 'Memory of My Father'. John Gawsworth, the London poet and anthologist, who read the 150-odd pieces Kavanagh had accumulated since the mid-1930s, was altogether less discriminating. Together, and separately, they assembled at least six collections, none of which was published. Ten years later, Kavanagh would scribble on a batch of poems in one of these 1930s collections, 'All unpub. all rightly so.'[10]

1939–46

By spring 1939 Kavanagh was determined to abandon farming and become a professional writer. He was back in London from April, looking for work as a reviewer and trying his hand at a novel, *The Land Remains*. Michael Joseph, publisher of *The Green Fool*, had an option on this novel but had offered no advance, feeling that he was owed £400 since the libel case. The penniless would-be novelist petitioned Harold Macmillan for employment and was offered a weekly retainer provided he could free himself of Joseph. When Joseph refused, Kavanagh could not afford to stay on in London.

That August, instead of returning to Mucker, Kavanagh moved to Dublin to live on a temporary basis with his young brother Peter, a teacher, and turn out a potboiler to fulfil his obligation to Joseph. The outbreak of war the following month prevented any return to London. *Faute de mieux*, he became a Dublin-based freelance writer. During his first three years in Dublin, he attempted to survive on the pittance he earned from reviewing regularly for the *Irish Times* and publishing the odd poem or feature article. (There was a short reprieve from this hand-to-mouth existence when he was the recipient of the first AE literary award of £100 in January 1940.) A morning writer, he spent his afternoons hunting unsuccessfully for a white-collar job and his evenings in the Palace Bar, the pub where writers and artists gathered. His frugal upbringing meant that he had not yet acquired a taste for alcohol, so he frequented the Palace for the conversation and the contacts, familiarizing himself with the opinions and attitudes of Dublin's literati. After a few years he had absorbed whatever he could learn from them and familiarity bred the contempt he later voiced in 'The Paddiad'.

Kavanagh would come to view the Palace set as 'the dregs of the old Literary Revival',[11] 'fusty, safe and dim' writers still preoccupied with producing a distinctively ethnic Irish literature long after political independence had been achieved. By contrast, Frank O'Connor and Sean O'Faolain, two Cork-born writers of his own age who had befriended Kavanagh, envisaged a documentary, 'condition of Ireland' literature, reporting the diversity of life in the Free State. In their opinion, the romantic, idealistic era just past was to be succeeded by a period of disillusioned realism. Yeats had died in 1939 and when O'Faolain became the founding editor of a new literary journal, *The Bell*, in 1940 and co-opted O'Connor as poetry editor, his first editorial set out his post-Yeatsian programme for

Irish letters. The writer's aim was no longer to boost national and nationalist morale but to record his own experience of life in Ireland. *The Bell*'s socio-realist aesthetic offered the floundering Kavanagh an artistic programme.

He broke with the *Dublin Magazine* after 1939 and the first number of *The Bell* carried his poem 'Stony Grey Soil'. He was also working on a new novel about small-farm life entitled *Stony Grey Soil*, with an anti-clerical plot suggested to him by O'Faolain. It had the kind of hero approved by the two Cork men, a young farmer whose aspirations are stifled by the realities of life in Ireland, compelled to marry a woman he does not love for the sake of her dowry.

During 1940–41 Kavanagh published a series of lyrics based on his childhood and on his adult years as a farmer in Inniskeen: affectionate, yet indecorously realist poems which include images of 'old buckets, rusty-holed', 'the hen's rooting where the sow scratches', 'barrels of blue potato-spray', cleaning out the cart after a day spent transporting dung. He was reading W. H. Auden and was excited by his fresh, sharp images. His own lyrics were too true to life even for O'Faolain, who felt they lacked polish and refinement. 'Kavanagh doesn't wash his poetry's ears,' he complained.[12] The customary gap between Kavanagh's poetry and fiction was now closing and his new lyrics were peopled poems in which 'a world comes to life'. This overlap between fiction and poetry shows in the use of the same title, 'Stony Grey Soil', for a poem and novel, but it is most evident in his crossing of the two genres in the novella-poems, *Why Sorrow?* and *The Great Hunger*. Each focuses on the secret frustrations of an elderly celibate, a priest-farmer in one, a bachelor farmer in the other, both living a double life, outwardly successful and inwardly tormented. In these long poems Kavanagh experiments with an irregular mix of free verse paragraphs and rhymed stanzas, a structure that was possibly influenced by *The Waste Land. Why Sorrow?* survives only in fragmentary form; *The Great Hunger* has come to be regarded as one of the finest long poems of the twentieth century.

The Great Hunger teems with images of country life at different seasons of the year and times of the day, offering a shockingly honest and comprehensive portrayal of a subsistence farmer's life. Kavanagh's technique is cinematic, cutting from scene to scene and zooming in on telling details, compressing a lifetime of procrastination and frustration into 759 lines. Patrick Maguire, the poem's anti-hero, is a pathetic figure, brutalized, even vegetized, by a fourteen-hour working day; an elderly wifeless and childless man, who 'lives that his little fields may stay fertile', sacrificing sexuality to agricultural productivity. He is timid, cautious, passive, a victim of the small-farm ethos embodied by his mother, in which success in life is measured in terms of high crop-yields, pre-marital chastity and regular attendance at Mass and confession. In foregrounding the plight of the bachelor farmer, Kavanagh was confronting one of the most crucial sociological issues in Ireland at this period: the 1936 census figures, released in 1938, had exposed the decline and depopulation of the countryside through late marriage and failure to marry.

The poem is at its most devastating in its assault on the cherished nationalist fiction of Irish spiritual ascendancy which was largely centred on peasant Ireland. With oracular authority, Kavanagh announces the victory of materialism over spirituality in 'every corner of this land', opening and closing his poem with an 'apocalypse of clay', a shocking perversion of Christ's incarnation. *The Great Hunger* also establishes a vital connection between spirituality and sexuality, generally presented as conflicting drives in contemporary Irish religious discourse. Kavanagh's God is one who delights in love and lust but has been distorted into a custodian of extramarital chastity. The poem's title and the recurrent motif of potato-harvesting suggest a disturbing analogy between the psycho-sexual deprivation that is depopulating and devitalizing contemporary Ireland and the famine that ravaged the country in the mid-nineteenth century. Now the potato crop flourishes, but human lives are blighted.

The Great Hunger is a didactic poem with palpable designs on the reader. It consciously sets out to subvert the cult of primitivism common in country-based poetry since the time of the *Lyrical Ballads*, as well as undermining the small-farm Utopia envisaged by Éamon de Valera, Ireland's Taoiseach. Towards the end of his life, Kavanagh would repudiate *The Great Hunger* because of its sociological concern with the 'woes of the poor'.[13] By then he had long since outgrown *The Bell*'s socio-realist aesthetic. When it was first published in 1942, however, the poem was remarkable not only for its political and poetic radicalism and its technical daring but for its personal courage. The 'ploughman poet' was demolishing the peasant myth which had given him his entrée to the world of Irish letters.

Lough Derg, Kavanagh's third and last long poem, dates from July 1942. In this poetic documentary on a three-day pilgrimage to St Patrick's Purgatory, he broadens his cultural analysis to present an anatomy of Catholic Ireland, urban and rural, North and South, poor and middle-class. The poem is biased against the middle classes and lenient towards the needy poor, shaping their prayers into sonnets. *Lough Derg* may have been included in the collection *A Satirical Pilgrimage*, rejected in 1944 by the Cuala Press, the publisher of *The Great Hunger*, and the following year by Faber.[14] It was only posthumously printed. However, as 'Advent' reveals, Kavanagh was having doubts about his socio-analytic programme by December 1942 and there were to be no further poems in this vein.

That October he finally secured regular employment as a twice-weekly gossip columnist with a large-circulation daily, the *Irish Press*. His column, written under the pen-name Piers Plowman, often included snatches of verse, usually light and topical. At the same time he was opening hostilities against the Literary Revival writers, Synge, Lady Gregory and Yeats, in a series of book reviews for a Catholic weekly, the *Standard*, asserting that, as writers from a Protestant Ascendancy caste, they were outside the mainstream consciousness of the Irish, were not 'the voice of the people'. Already, he was jousting for top place in the Irish literary pantheon and he would continue to challenge the hegemony of the Literary Revival for the rest of his life. By spring 1944 he was once again unemployed and his disenchantment with Dublin began to surface in 'Pegasus' and 'A Wreath for Tom Moore's Statue'. The following year two arch-bishops[15] came to his rescue and he was appointed staff journalist and, from 1946, film critic on the *Standard*.

The poetry of the war years was collected in *A Soul for Sale* (1947), submitted to Macmillan in 1945. The early submission date meant that it excluded two of his best-known 1940s poems, the elegy 'In Memory of My Mother' and the popular love song 'On Raglan Road'. It was Kavanagh's first mature collection and the first time *The Great Hunger*, which had been published in a limited edition, was widely available. This long poem proved controversial because it challenged literary pieties about peasantry and was so technically innovative, yet many of his fellow-writers saluted its imaginative power. Kavanagh was now acknowledged as a force to be reckoned with in Irish letters.

1947–55

By the late 1940s Kavanagh was looked on by Dubliners as a 'charac-ter'. His job as staff reporter on the *Standard* had lasted only two years and he had reverted to being a morning writer who usually spent the rest of the day in town. Tall, thin and unkempt, he was a familiar figure in his battered hat and horn-rimmed spectacles, muttering to himself as he walked and occasionally kicking out at imaginary obstacles. He had moved to his long-term residence, an apartment at 62 Pembroke Road, in 1943, and the surrounding area, which he called his 'Pembrokeshire', gradually took over from Inniskeen as his village. Many of the large Georgian houses in this part of Dublin were divided into apartments occupied by young married couples or office workers. He enjoyed the hospitality of some of the married couples and chatted up pretty single women, taking an interest in their jobs and romances. He was also known for his kindly way with children, telling them stories and giving them sweets. Towards adults who presumed an unwanted familiarity, his rudeness became legendary. Living too much in the public eye, he protected himself against intrusiveness by terse, growled insults or snarled requests for money. He seemed determined to exaggerate his difference from his fellow-writers, generally a neatly dressed, middle-class and mannerly group. To those he befriended, he was an entertaining and endearing man; to those he deliberately alienated, a monster.

From 1947 Kavanagh resumed his association with *The Bell* under its new editor, Peadar O'Donnell, novelist and socialist. His first contribution was an elegy for the Labour leader Jim Larkin. O'Donnell serialized Kavanagh's novel *Tarry Flynn* and puffed its author. This novel had started out as *Stony Grey Soil* seven years previously, had been revised and resubmitted as *Mother and Children* to Macmillan and Methuen in 1944 and, finally, stripped of its anti-clerical plot and unhappy ending, emerged as a lyrical yet comic portrait of the artist as a young farmer. Published by the Pilot Press, London, in 1948, its shelf-life was short because the publishers went into liquidation a year later. Though it was a critical success from the first, its present status as a classic of Irish country life was established only when it began to be republished from 1962.

The verse playlet 'The Wake of the Books', in the November 1947 issue of *The Bell*, inaugurated a new phase in Kavanagh's writing, a period of sustained cultural criticism. Over the coming years he would often resort to dramatic techniques when travestying attitudes to the arts in Dublin: his characters condemn themselves out of their own mouths in dramas, dramatic monologues or passages of dialogue within a poem. 'The Wake of the Books', however, makes little or no coherent contribution to its ostensible subject, the debate over the draconian application of the Irish Censorship Act of 1929. Censorship never interested Kavanagh; here he is just as concerned with the attitudes of potential patrons and hangers-on in the arts world and with poetry as an antidote to their jaded cynicism. When *The Bell* suspended publication for lack of funding in 1949, John Ryan, the editor of a new monthly periodical, *Envoy*, offered him a platform to air his views on literature and culture in a column entitled 'Diary'. Among his chief targets in this lively and often outrageous column were 'the pygmy literature of the Literary Revival' and the still prevalent literary obsession with Irishness in theme and technique. So vehement was his opposition to the use of Irishness as an aesthetic criterion that he more than once asserted, 'Irishness is a form of anti-art.'[16]

In a spate of satiric verse published in *Envoy* and elsewhere, he voiced his disdain for Dublin as a cultural capital, railing against its literary cliques ('Jungle', 'The Paddiad'), its substitution of literary chit-chat in the pub for the hard graft of writing ('Tale of Two Cities'), its cult of actors and film stars ('Adventure in the Bohemian Jungle'), government patronage of the arts ('Irish Stew') and the Arts Council ('Prelude'). 'The Christmas Mummers' satirizes a peculiarly Irish go-getter mentality which manipulates national sentiment and the cult of ethnicity in its scramble for self-advancement. Patriotism is shown to be the first refuge of the Irish scoundrel. Kavanagh draws on defamiliarizing tropes in these satires: Dublin is a jungle or, in 'The Defeated', a piggery. A recurrent trope is Dublin as hell, devoted to the worship of second-rate art. In 'The Paddiad', set in a literary pub reminiscent of the Palace or Pearl Bar, Irish poetry is presided over by the polite, smooth-talking devil Mediocrity. His antithesis, Paddy Conscience, with his 'drunken talk and dirty clothes', bears a striking resemblance to Paddy Kavanagh. Indeed, he is often recognizable as the hero of his satires: an outsider and outcast, appalled by Ireland's complacent, self-congratulatory sense of its cultural importance. In 'Adventure in the Bohemian Jungle' he is identifiable as the 'man from the mythical land of simple country', literally nauseated by the alliance between big business, show business and the Catholic Church.

Sometimes, as in 'The Hero' (originally 'Dublin'), the city is belittled by the depiction of the poet narrator as a giant among pygmies, Gulliver in Lilliput, a godlike figure towering above mere mortals. The satires were introvertedly local. Addressed to an Irish and mainly Dublin readership, they did not travel well. The best of them, 'The Paddiad', was rejected by *Poetry* (Chicago); Cyril Connolly, who took it for his London monthly, *Horizon*, was familiar with Dublin's Palace Bar. Kavanagh was wary of his own aptitude for satire, seeing it as inimical to his lyrical gift, diminishing him spiritually: it was 'unfruitful prayer'. Several poems of this period thematize the quarrel within his own psyche between satire and love.

Fortunately, just as he seemed about to typecast himself as a perpetually earnest and outraged prig in his verse, he discovered a more multi-dimensional role, the self as character rather than moral exemplar. He began to write humorous, vernacular, confessional poems in which the self is portrayed as a combination of fallible human person (often an unsuccessful lover) and dedicated poet. In 'Bank Holiday', 'Auditors In' and 'Prelude', even in 'If Ever You Go to Dublin Town', he takes the reader into his confidence, revealing himself to be a remarkably honest and shrewd self-analyst, alert to the pitfalls of his own temperament and circumstances. Instead of condemning Dublin's devilry, he is intent on casting out his own demons. The scolding tones of Mrs Flynn berating her lazy, errant son, Tarry, are now internalized. Because it was so intimate and involved so much exposure both of his own unsaintly character and of his reverence for the poet in himself, this was a risky poetry to publish in a small, gossipy society like Dublin. It would never have occurred to him to conceal his high romantic view of the poet's status: whether 'poor or pushed around', the poet was always to Kavanagh a prophet, a visionary, a theologian, a god. It infuriated him that so many other Irish writers laid spurious claim to this elevated status. 'The standing army of Irish poets' seldom falls below 10,000, he commented sardonically.[17]

In the satires Kavanagh had shown a talent for mimicry and

ventriloquism; in the self-portraits he evolves a personal speaking voice that can modulate from the argot of street, racetrack and boxing ring to literary and religious allusion, or take off from near-doggerel to 'soar in summer air'. Above all, he writes as a modern urban man, incidentally not programmatically Irish. Although he might still look like a 'peasant' and would never lose his south Monaghan accent, his intellectual sophistication, wry humour and, perhaps unexpectedly, his literariness are now displayed.

One of the topics Kavanagh explores in the 1950s is the creative process, the 'God of imagination waking'. While 'Epic', 'Auditors In', 'On Reading a Book on Common Wild Flowers' and 'Kerr's Ass' associate the workings of imagination with a return to his country past, these are poems about the legitimate themes of poetry or the psychic states conducive to creativity, not descriptive rural lyrics.

In the first half of the 1950s most of Kavanagh's poetry was published in *Envoy* during its twenty-month existence from December 1949, in the revived *Bell*, when his friend Anthony Cronin was Associate Editor, and in *Kavanagh's Weekly*, the short-lived periodical he edited and co-wrote with his brother, Peter Kavanagh, from 12 April to 5 July 1952. *Kavanagh's Weekly* mounted a vigorous assault against many of the aspects of contemporary Irish life that angered him: among them the Fianna Fáil government under the leadership of de Valera; state-sponsored bodies involved in the arts, especially Radio Éireann, the Abbey Theatre and the Arts Council; the materialism, philistinism and smug chauvinism of the Irish. Most weeks a poem was included, but, apart from 'The Ghost Land', these poems are not concerned with social criticism, and they include the ironic autobiographical lyric 'I Had a Future' and the light-hearted 'A Ballad'. 'Having Confessed', with which the thirteen-week run of *Kavanagh's Weekly* concluded, is yet another of those poems where he abjures anger and indignation and seeks to cultivate a psychic state receptive to inspiration.

Kavanagh's Weekly was a breath of fresh air in Irish journalism, but it had antagonized so many sectors of Irish society that its ex-editor found himself virtually unemployable. For the next few years he was almost destitute, kept afloat by handouts from friends and well-wishers. He had taken to gambling on horses, another drain on his scant resources. As the sonnet 'Nineteen Fifty-Four' discloses, that year, in particular, was an *annus horribilis*. He was still unemployed, and when he took a libel action in the hope of making money he initially lost the case; that autumn a girlfriend he had been stringing along for over five years married someone else; he was also in poor health, complaining of shoulder pain and catarrh. Small wonder that he began to seek solace in whiskey and was soon frequently drunk. A heavy cigarette smoker all his life, he was diagnosed with lung cancer in March 1955 and had a lung removed. While he made a good, if slow, recovery, he never regained his former robustness. However, his years of near destitution were now over. An extra-mural lectureship was created for him at University College Dublin, which ensured him a modest monthly income. It was intended to be a sinecure but he delivered an annual spring series of poetry lectures for many years.

1956–9

After a lengthy convalescence, some of it spent lying on the bank of Dublin's Grand Canal in the warm July of 1955, Kavanagh was full of publishing plans. When the new selection of poems he sent to Macmillan in November was rejected, he was so hurt and downcast that a friend, the painter Patrick Swift, arranged with David Wright, editor of the literary quarterly *Nimbus*, to publish a mini-collection of nineteen poems. These duly appeared in the winter 1956 number with an appreciative introductory essay by Anthony Cronin, then literary editor of *Time and Tide*. It was Kavanagh's first post-war collection and included some of his best 1950s poems, 'Auditors In', 'Prelude', 'Epic' and 'Kerr's Ass', and also a new sonnet, 'The Hospital', which looks forward to his next poetic phase. John McGahern recalls the exhilaration the *Nimbus* collection aroused in young writers like himself, the feeling that 'literature could belong again to the streets rather than to the Church and university and the worn establishment'. From now on, the upcoming generation of Irish writers were 'all partisans'.[18]

Kavanagh spent the first half of 1957 in New York. Shortly after his return to Dublin, he announced that he was 'writing verse in a new style', a 'new kind of poem with new words'. Between late June and October he produced eighteen poems in this 'new mood', the group that begins with 'October' and ends with 'Winter' in the present collection. Though this poetry does not make a complete thematic or stylistic break with his previous verse, the outlook and mood are different. His 'noo pomes', as he called them, are more colourful and sensuous than usual, and are utterly celebratory.[19] Most are love poems to canal or street, country lane or cutaway bog. They are present-tense salutations, rapturously greeting the here and now or hailing the future with optimism. The style is vernacular, drawing on speech rhythms yet capable of modulating into prayer or rhapsody. Improvisatory techniques are exploited to convey an air of immediacy and spontaneity. Repetitions, even triple repetitions, which were a feature of his own speech when he was being emphatic, are quite common: 'praise, praise, praise'; 'beautiful, beautiful, beautiful God'. Rhyme is often foregrounded and the frequently off-chime and half-rhymes result in some deliberately incongruous couplings: 'person' with 'arsing'; 'thighs' with 'wise'; 'prose' with 'noise'. His aim is to write about 'casual, insignificant little things', to achieve a humorous, relaxed style, to play 'a true note on a dead slack string'.[20] Yet for all its apparent spontaneity and directness this verse has a 'shapely form': some of the lyrics are sonnets; others are written in couplets. Continuity with his earlier 1950s poetry is perhaps most obvious in the fact that many of the 'noo pomes' are poems about poetry: credos, manifestos, poetic stocktakings, announcements of future plans, glimpses of 'the muse at her toilet'.

He was so grateful for this unexpected surge of lyrical energy that he constructed a much-reiterated personal myth to enhance its significance, proclaiming that he had been born or reborn as a poet during his summer convalescence on the bank of Dublin's Grand Canal two years previously. While his near brush with death and his restoration to health and vitality after his cancer operation were profound psychic experiences, it is also probable that the six months he spent in New York had rejuvenated him imaginatively.

1960–67

Thirty-five lyrics, including the eighteen 'noo pomes', fourteen written between 1945 and 1955 and three early pieces, were collected in *Come Dance with Kitty Stobling and Other Poems*, published by Longmans, Green and Co. in spring 1960. (Sixteen of the 'noo pomes' had been included in a limited edition entitled *Recent Poems*, printed on his brother Peter's newly acquired hand press in 1958.) *Come Dance with Kitty Stobling*, especially the sonnets, received enthusiastic reviews and the collection was the Poetry Society's spring choice.

The following November the *Observer* carried 'News Item', a covert love poem to his future wife, Katherine Barry Moloney, whom he had met in London the previous year. Gibson Square in Islington where she then lived had become, like Raglan Road, an 'enchanted way'. The poem concludes 'I'm as happy as I've ever been.' The couple would marry in Dublin in April 1967.

For the last seven years of his life Kavanagh divided his time between Dublin, Katherine's apartment in London and the old family home in Inniskeen, now occupied by his two elder sisters, both nurses. A weekly column in the *Irish Farmers' Journal*, and afterwards in the *RTV Guide*, supplemented his small university salary. After 1960, as his drinking increased, his poetic output dwindled. He was by now frequently ill, subject to pneumonia and bronchitis and also, of course, to hangovers, stomach pains and nausea brought on by alcoholic excess. However, the casual, confessional poetic he had evolved enabled him to versify even such distressing circumstances. Indeed, it seems peculiarly appropriate to these last poems, bringing a tone of comic ruefulness to their sorry tale of alcoholic indignity and waning creativity. Where he had turned to W. H. Auden to modernize his poetry at the outset of his career, he was now excited by 'the fun and games' of Beat verse.[21] 'Let words laugh,' he wrote in 'Mermaid Tavern'. In practice, this resulted in a ludic emphasis on rhyme and sometimes a descent into doggerel. There was often a fine line between the carefree and the careless. Yet these late poems admit the whole adult self into poetry as never before, not compartmentalizing the satirist and celebrant or seeking to purify the abusive, opportunistic aspects of the self. The dread underlying the gaiety of his late writings is acknowledged in 'Personal Problem', the bleakest poem he ever wrote.

To the end of his life Kavanagh was dogged by comparisons with Yeats. 'Greatest Irish poet since Yeats', a phrase frequently applied to him, was, as he well knew, a euphemism for 'second best poet after Yeats'. He himself repeatedly squared up to Yeats, assessing him as poet and man in essays and reviews, often starting out with hostile intent, but usually compelled to honour his moral authority and to admire at least part of his œuvre. His ambivalence towards Yeats was not merely based upon literary competitiveness, what Harold Bloom termed 'the anxiety of influence'. As man and poet, Kavanagh was Yeats's antithesis, with his 'peasant' provenance and Catholic sensibility, his recoil from Irish nationalism, myth and history, his choice of 'common and banal' subjects and contemporary vernacular speech in poetry, even his love of sport and frequenting of pubs, betting shops, racetracks. While cherishing the sacredness of the poet's office, Kavanagh never lost the common touch. His enduring appeal for Irish readers is, undoubtedly, rooted in a recognition that he is one of ourselves.

Unfortunately, Kavanagh's only poem on Yeats, which is also the last poem he published, does scant justice to his complex lifelong relationship with the older poet. Here he envies the Yeats of 'Amongst Schoolchildren' his assured public status and safe, privileged lifestyle, feeling himself to be at sixty an undervalued outsider. A chronically insecure man, Kavanagh's insecurities were compounded by circumstance: a precarious livelihood as a freelance journalist, a nomadic, disorganized bachelor existence, the uncertainties attendant on publication and reviews, the highs and lows that went with gambling and alcoholism.

He still dreamed that he would moderate his drinking, rally his flagging energies and enjoy another productive season, but it was not to be. Nevertheless, during the last years of his life Kavanagh experienced the literary success that had come his way only rarely and at long intervals hitherto. Thanks to Timothy O'Keeffe of Mac-Gibbon & Kee, who had taken over as his publisher, most of his writings, except *The Green Fool* which he refused permission to reissue, were in print. *Collected Poems* appeared in 1964, *Collected Pruse* in 1967 and a hardback edition of *Tarry Flynn* in 1965. The Abbey Theatre's version of *Tarry Flynn*, staged in December 1966, was a box-office success. He was almost as well known in Soho as in Dublin, and in October 1967 was given a British Arts Council award. In Ireland, he received no state recognition or state-sponsored subsidy: 'He never qualified for a directorship or a State pension,' as he put it in 'No Social Conscience'. Official neglect was, to some extent, compensated for by public esteem. He was surrounded by friends and well-wishers, widely regarded as Ireland's leading poet, lionized by university students and the upcoming generation of poets. Perhaps the supreme accolade for a poet who once wrote 'If roots I had they were in the school books' was to have his own poetry placed on the Irish secondary school curriculum in June 1967.[22] There was much for which to say 'Thank You, Thank You':

> For most have died the day before
> The opening of that holy door.

Patrick Kavanagh died in a Dublin nursing home on 30 November 1967 and was buried in Inniskeen.

Notes

(A broad selection of Patrick Kavanagh's essays and journalism is reprinted in Patrick Kavanagh, *A Poet's Country: Selected Prose*, ed. Antoinette Quinn, The Lilliput Press, Dublin, 2003, here abbreviated to *APC*.)

1. Ms 3215, National Library of Ireland.
2. *The Green Fool*, p. 260.
3. 'Literature in the University', *Envoy*, July 1951, *APC*, p. 233.
4. ibid.
5. 'Return in Harvest', *The Bell*, April 1954, *APC*, p. 106.
6. Daniel Corkery, *Synge and Anglo-Irish Literature* (1931), p. 15, on the disadvantage of a colonial literary education for the Irish poet.
7. The normal term in Ireland was 'small farmer' rather than 'peasant'; 'peasant' was current as a literary term but would otherwise have been considered condescending.
8. 'A Strange Irish Poet', *Irish Times*, 30 and 31 March 1945.
9. *Self-Portrait* (1964), *APC*, p. 306.
10. Ms 3215, National Library of Ireland.
11. 'From Monaghan to the Grand Canal', *Studies*, Spring 1959, *APC*, p. 275.
12. O'Faolain/O'Connor correspondence, Boston City University Library.
13. Author's Note to *Collected Poems* (1964). See Appendix A.
14. Ann Saddlemyer, *Becoming George, The Life of Mrs W. B. Yeats*, Oxford University Press, 2002, p. 593.
15. The Archbishop of Dublin, John Charles McQuaid, was to prove a lifelong benefactor; the Archbishop of Tuam, Joseph Walsh, befriended the poet at this time.
16. 'On a Liberal Education', *X*, vol. ii, no. 2, August 1961, *APC*, p. 291, and *Self-Portrait*, *APC*, p. 309.
17. See note on 'The Christmas Mummers'.
18. John McGahern, *Evening Herald*, July 1987, and 'The Solitary Reader', *Canadian Journal of Irish Studies*, July 1991.
19. His comments on this poetry are in letters to Peter Kavanagh, dated 6 July, 14 October and 5 December 1957, Kavanagh Archive, University College,

Dublin, published in Peter Kavanagh (ed.), *Lapped Furrows*, Peter Kavanagh
Handpress, New York, 1969, pp. 202, 203, 206.

20. *Self-Portrait, APC*, pp. 311, 313, 315.

21. In an interview with Máirín O'Farrell, *Hibernia*, May 1964; 'I like Corso,
Ferlinghetti and Allen Ginsberg very much'; also *Tri-quarterly*, no. 4, 1965.

22. 'School Book Poetry', *Kavanagh's Weekly*, 10 May 1952, *APC*, p. 270.

Editorial Note

Poems in this volume have been selected with the aim of presenting the best of Patrick Kavanagh's poetry. However, some inferior verse is included because it represents a particular phase or propensity in his œuvre and, for the same reasons, the fragmentary long poem *Why Sorrow?* is collected, despite the fact that some stanzas or versions of them appear in two poems quarried from it, 'The Long Garden' and 'Father Mat'.

Collected Poems follows the chronology of first publication, except for poems first published in *Collected Poems* (1964) or posthumously, which are listed according to the manuscript date, and some poems from an unpublished collection of 1955. On account of the lengthy interval between the publication of *Ploughman and Other Poems* (1936), *A Soul for Sale* (1947) and *Come Dance with Kitty Stobling and Other Poems* (1960) and the number of interesting poems they exclude, it was decided not to base the volume on these three collections. Instead, the poems are arranged in five chronological groupings. While these do not represent five distinct phases in Kavanagh's poetic career and certain similarities will be apparent, especially between poems that occur towards the end of one and the beginning of the next, in general they do illustrate changing trends in his verse.

The first, 1929–38, begins with his first published poems and is largely based on *Ploughman and Other Poems* (1936) and the two manuscript collections *The Seed and the Soil* (1937) and *To Anna Quinn* (1938), subtitled Second Poems and Third Poems respectively. During this phase Kavanagh was experimenting with different poetic models and styles and producing verse for both a British and an Irish market. An unfortunate consequence of following chronology in this instance is that the first poems the new reader confronts are among Kavanagh's weakest. Even at this early stage, however, there are a few fine lyrics, such as 'Inniskeen Road: July Evening' and 'Shancoduff'. The second group, 1939–46, opens in the year that the poet definitively turned his back on the career of farmer. Though his move to Dublin in August 1939 and the outbreak of the Second World War the following month had no immediate effect on Kavanagh's poetry, a gradual change becomes apparent as he begins writing primarily for an Irish audience and evoking life in a farming community. War is an intermittent background presence in these poems. From 1947 to 1955 most of Kavanagh's poems were published in the Irish monthly magazines *The Bell* and *Envoy*, in his own short-lived weekly, *Kavanagh's Weekly*, or in the *Irish Times* newspaper, which had been printing his work since 1935. A few languished unpublished in a 1955 collection rejected by Macmillan, the publisher of his two previous collections. During these years, satires on Dublin's literary and cultural milieu are interspersed with poems abjuring satire or returning to country life for inspiration and with self-portraits and analyses of his own creative processes. Between 1956 and 1959 Kavanagh experienced a new creative surge when, following on his recovery from an operation for lung cancer, he produced some of his best lyrics and proclaimed himself born-again as a poet. It was also a period when he published or republished extensively in London – nineteen poems in *Nimbus*, five in *Encounter*, two in *Time and Tide*, two in *X* – and it culminated in the award-winning, London-published collection *Come Dance with Kitty Stobling and Other Poems* (1960). Thereafter – 1960–67 – the decline in creativity, which became one of his recurring themes, was sometimes accompanied by a new outrageousness in the matter and manner of his verse, a wilful impropriety in tone and content and a liking for doggerel rhymes.

Kavanagh revised many of his poems between journal and book publication. This edition follows the text of *Ploughman and Other Poems*, *A Soul for Sale* and *Come Dance with Kitty Stobling and Other Poems*, with the exception of *The Great Hunger*, where it follows the Cuala Press text of 1942 rather than the bowdlerized version printed in *A Soul for Sale*. For poems not included in these three collections, I have returned to the magazine version or, with unpublished poems, the manuscript version. An exception has been made in the case of those magazine poems revised for an unpublished 1955 collection, where I follow the revised version. Untitled manuscript poems have been entitled from the opening words of the poem.

The date and place of first publication and the source text for poems are given in the Notes. As the prefatory 'Author's Note' to his *Collected Poems* (1964) makes clear, Kavanagh had no input into this collection which offers numerous variant readings on published and manuscript texts, so I have not used it as a source text.

Certain spellings have been standardized/modernized throughout this edition. Punctuation, which is sometimes quite erratic (particularly in Kavanagh's magazine and manuscript poems), has been regularized, though with a minimum of interference. Otherwise, those rare instances where the text deviates from the source text (e.g. the correction of an obvious misprint) are flagged in the Notes.

Hundreds of poems are not collected here. Most of these are low-grade apprentice verses dating from six early collections unpublished in Kavanagh's lifetime. With a few exceptions, the 'light verse' from his City Commentary column in the *Irish Press* (1942–4) is also omitted, as are many of his occasional pieces and a sprinkling of other poems and fragments which he did not collect or, in some cases, publish. Anyone wishing to read these uncollected poems will find them on the website of the Trustees of the Estate of the late Katherine B. Kavanagh, www.*tcd.ie/English/patrickkavanagh*.

The Poems

1929–38

Address to an Old Wooden Gate

Battered by time and weather, scarcely fit
For firewood; there's not a single bit
Of paint to hide those wrinkles, and such scringes
Break hoarsely on the silence – rusty hinges:
A barbed wire clasp around one withered arm
Replaces the old latch, with evil charm.
That poplar tree you hang upon is rotten,
And all its early loveliness forgotten.
This gap ere long must find another sentry
If the cows are not to roam the open country.
They'll laugh at you, Old Wooden Gate, they'll push
Your limbs asunder, soon, into the slush.
Then I will lean upon your top no more
To muse, and dream of pebbles on a shore,
Or watch the fairy-columned turf-smoke rise
From white-washed cottage chimneys heaven-wise.
Here have I kept fair tryst, and kept it true,
When we were lovers all, and you were new;
And many a time I've seen the laughing-eyed
Schoolchildren, on your trusty back astride.
But Time's long silver hand has touched our brows,
And I'm the scorned of women – you of cows.
How can I love the iron gates which guard
The fields of wealthy farmers? They are hard,
Unlovely things, a-swing on concrete piers –
Their finger-tips are pointed like old spears.
But you and I are kindred, Ruined Gate,
For both of us have met the self-same fate.

Patrick Kavanagh

The Intangible

Rapt to starriness – not quite,
I go through fields and fens of night,
The nameless, the void,
Where ghostly poplars whisper to
A silent countryside.

Not black or blue,
Grey or red or tan,
The skies I travel under.
A strange unquiet wonder.
Indian
Vision and thunder.

Splendours of Greek,
Egypt's cloud-woven glory,
Speak no more, speak,
Speak no more
A thread-worn story.

Ploughman

I turn the lea-green down
Gaily now,
And paint the meadow brown
With my plough.

I dream with silvery gull
And brazen crow.
A thing that is beautiful
I may know.

Tranquillity walks with me
And no care.
O, the quiet ecstasy
Like a prayer.

I find a star-lovely art
In a dark sod.
Joy that is timeless! O heart
That knows God!

To a Blackbird

O pagan poet, you
And I are one
In this – we lose our god
At set of sun.

And we are kindred when
The hill wind shakes
Sweet song like blossoms on
The calm green lakes.

We dream while Earth's sad children
Go slowly by
Pleading for our conversion
With the Most High.

Gold Watch

Engraved on the case,
House and mountain
And a far mist
Rising from faery fountain.

On inner case,
No. 2244
Elgin Nath . . .
Sold by a guy in a New York store.

Dates of repairs,
1914 M. Y., 1918 H. J.,
She has had her own cares.

Slender hands
Of blue steel,
And within the precious
Platinum balance wheel.

Delicate mechanism
Counting out in her counting-house
My pennies of time.

Beech Tree

I planted in February
A bronze-leafed beech,
In the chill brown soil
I spread out its silken fibres.

Protected it from the goats
With wire netting,
And fixed it firm against
The worrying wind.

Now it is safe, I said,
April must stir
My precious baby
To greenful loveliness.

It is August now, I have hoped,
But I hope no more –
My beech tree will never hide sparrows
From hungry hawks.

To a Child

Child, do not go
Into the dark places of soul,
For there the grey wolves whine,
The lean grey wolves.

I have been down
Among the unholy ones who tear
Beauty's white robe and clothe her
In rags of prayer.

Child, there is light somewhere
Under a star.
Sometime it will be for you
A window that looks
Inward to God.

My Room

10 by 12
And a low roof,
If I stand by the side wall
My head feels the reproof.

Five holy pictures
Hang on the walls –
The Virgin and Child,
St Anthony of Padua,
St Patrick our own,
Leo XIII
And the Little Flower.

My bed in the centre,
So many things to me –
A dining table,
A writing desk,
A couch,
And a slumber palace.

My room is a musty attic,
But its little window
Lets in the stars.

Four Birds

Kestrel

In a sky ballroom
The kestrel,
A stately dancer.
He is a true artist –
His art is not divorced
From life
And death.

Owl

Night-winged
As a ghost
Or a gangster,
Mystical as a black priest
Reading the Devil's Mass.

Lark

Morning star
Announcing the birth
Of a love-child.

Corn-crake

A cry in the wilderness
Of meadow.

To a Late Poplar

Not yet half-drest,
O tardy bride!
And the priest
And the bridegroom and the guests
Have been waiting a full hour.

The meadow choir
Is playing the wedding march
Two fields away,
And squirrels are already leaping in ecstasy
Among leaf-full branches.

After May

May came, and every shabby phoenix flapped
A coloured rag in lieu of shining wings;
In school bad manners spat and went unslapped –
Schoolmistress Fancy dreamt of other things.
The lilac blossomed for a day or two
Gaily, and then grew weary of her fame.
Plough-horses out on grass could now pursue
The pleasures of the very mute and tame.

A light that might be mystic or a fraud
Played on far hills beyond all common sight,
And some men said that it was Adam's God
As Adam saw before the Apple-bite.
Sweet May is gone, and now must poets croon
The praises of a rather stupid June.

Tinker's Wife

I saw her amid the dunghill debris
Looking for things
Such as an old pair of shoes or gaiters.
She was a young woman,
A tinker's wife.
Her face had streaks of care
Like wires across it,
But she was supple
As a young goat
On a windy hill.

She searched on the dunghill debris,
Tripping gingerly
Over tin canisters
And sharp-broken
Dinner plates.

April

Now is the hour we rake out the ashes
Of the spirit-fires winter-kindled.
This old temple must fall,
We dare not leave it
Dark, unlovely, deserted.
Level! O level it down!
Here we are building a bright new town.

That old cranky spinster is dead
Who fed us cold flesh.
And in the green meadows
The maiden of Spring is with child
By the Holy Ghost.

Inniskeen Road: July Evening

The bicycles go by in twos and threes –
There's a dance in Billy Brennan's barn tonight,
And there's the half-talk code of mysteries
And the wink-and-elbow language of delight.
Half-past eight and there is not a spot
Upon a mile of road, no shadow thrown
That might turn out a man or woman, not
A footfall tapping secrecies of stone.

I have what every poet hates in spite
Of all the solemn talk of contemplation.
Oh, Alexander Selkirk knew the plight
Of being king and government and nation.
A road, a mile of kingdom, I am king
Of banks and stones and every blooming thing.

March

The trees were in suspense,
Listening with an intense
Anxiety for the Word
That in the Beginning stirred
The dark-branched Tree
Of Humanity.

Subjectively the dogs
Hunted the muted bogs,
The horses suppressed their neighing,
No donkey-kind was braying,
The hare and rabbit under-
Stood the cause of wonder.

The blackbird of the yew
Alone broke the two
Minutes' silence
With a new poem's violence.
A tomboy scare that drove
Faint thoughts to active love.

Sanctity

To be a poet and not know the trade,
To be a lover and repel all women;
Twin ironies by which great saints are made,
The agonizing pincer-jaws of Heaven.

Monaghan Hills

Monaghan hills,
You have made me the sort of man I am,
A fellow who can never care a damn
For Everestic thrills.

The country of my mind
Has a hundred little heads,
On none of which foot-room for genius.

Because of you I am a half-faithed ploughman,
Shallow furrows at my heels,
Because of you I am a beggar of song
And a coward in thunder.

If I had been born among the Mournes,
Even in Forkhill,
I might have had echo-corners in my soul
Repeating the dawn laughter.

I might have climbed to know the glory
Of toppling from the roof of seeing –
O Monaghan hills, when is writ your story,
A carbon-copy will unfold my being.

The Hired Boy

Let me be no wiser than the dull
And leg-dragged boy who wrought
For John Maguire in Donaghmoyne
With never a vain thought
For fortune waiting round the next
Blind turning of Life's lane;
In dreams he never married a lady
To be dreamed-divorced again.

He knew what he wanted to know –
How the best potatoes are grown
And how to put flesh on a York pig's back
And clay on a hilly bone.
And how to be satisfied with the little
The destiny masters give
To the beasts of the tillage country –
To be damned and yet to live.

My People

Stranger:
What kind your people are
I would wish to know:
Great-shouldered men like rolling stock,
Great in despair,
Simple in prayer,
And their hard hands tear
The soil on the rock
Where the plough cannot go?

Poet:
'Tis not so.
Faint-hearted folk my people are,
To Poverty's house they have never invited
The giant Pride,
But await the world where wrongs are righted.
They till their fields and scrape among the stones
Because they cannot be schoolmasters –
They work because Judge Want condemns the drones.
Dear stranger, duty is a joke
Among my peasant folk.

Stranger:
Poet be fair,
You surely must have seen
Beneath these rags of care
Hearts that were not mean
And beggarly and faint.

Poet:
O curious stranger, why
Should poet seek to prove
The spirit of a saint?
For one in love
Would never probe or pry
Into the mysteried cove
Where all that is God's
Is safe from the hurtling clods.
I cannot tell you what you ask
But I will tell you other things –
I will fill the flask
Of your curiosity with bitterings.

Stranger:
I will go
To my town back again
And never desire to know
The hearts of your women and men.

Poet:
Our women are humble as dust,
They suck the hard crust,
They suckle our children, and we
Drink the milk of love's mystery.

Stranger:
I will go
To my townful of vermin
That sways to and fro
Like fool-heads at a sermon.
I will pour out for them
Your vitriol of hell.

And may Christ condemn
My name if I tell
The dream of your folk
That arose as you spoke.

Shancoduff

My black hills have never seen the sun rising,
Eternally they look north towards Armagh.
Lot's wife would not be salt if she had been
Incurious as my black hills that are happy
When dawn whitens Glassdrummond chapel.

My hills hoard the bright shillings of March
While the sun searches in every pocket.
They are my Alps and I have climbed the Matterhorn
With a sheaf of hay for three perishing calves
In the field under the Big Forth of Rocksavage.

The sleety winds fondle the rushy beards of Shancoduff
While the cattle-drovers sheltering in the Featherna Bush
Look up and say: 'Who owns them hungry hills
That the water-hen and snipe must have forsaken?
A poet? Then by heavens he must be poor.'
I hear and is my heart not badly shaken?

April Dusk

April dusk.
It is tragic to be a poet now
And not a lover
Paradised under the mutest bough.

I look through my window and see
The ghost of life flitting bat-winged.
O I am as old as a sage can ever be,
O I am as lonely as the first fool kinged.

The horse in his stall turns away
From the hay-filled manger, dreaming of grass
Soft and cool in hollows. O does he neigh
Jealousy-words for John MacGuigan's ass
That never was civilized in stall or trace?

An unmusical ploughboy whistles down the lane,
Not worried at all about the fate of Europe,
While I sit here feeling the subtle pain
That every silenced poet has endured.

Poplar Memory

I walked under the autumned poplars that my father planted
On a day in April when I was a child
Running beside the heap of suckers
From which he picked the straightest, most promising.

My father dreamt forests, he is dead –
And there are poplar forests in the waste-places
And on the banks of drains.

When I look up
I see my father
Peering through the branched sky.

Poet

Winter encloses me.
I am fenced,
The light, the laugh, the dance
Against.

I am like a monk
In a grey cell
Copying out my soul's
Queer miracle.

What goes on out there
In the light
Is less than a blue-bottle's flirtation.
Yet spite!

I would be a blue-bottle
Or a house-fly
And let the monk, the task,
In darkness lie.

Pursuit of an Ideal

November is come and I wait for you still,
O nimble-footed nymph who slipped me when
I sighted you among some silly men
And charged you with the power of my will.
Headlong I charged to make a passionate kill,
Too easy, far too easy, I cried then,
You were not worth one drop from off my pen.
O flower of the common light, the thrill
Of common things raised up to angelhood
Leaped in your flirt-wild legs. I followed you
Through April, May and June into September,
And still you kept your lead till passion's food
Went stale within my satchel. Now I woo
The footprints that you make across November.

In the Same Mood

You will not always be far away and pure
As a word conceived in a poet's silver womb.
You will not always be a metaphysical signature
To all the poems I write. In my bleak room
This very year by God's will you may be
A woman innocent in her first sin
Having cast off the immortality
Of the never-to-be-born. The violin
Is not more real than the music played upon it.
They told me that, the priests – but I am tired
Of loving through the medium of a sonnet;
I want by Man, not God, to be inspired.
This year, O maiden of the dream-vague face,
You'll come to me, a thing of Time and Space.

The Irony of It

I have not the fine audacity of men
Who have mastered the pen
Or the purse.
The complexes of many slaves are in my verse.
When I straighten my shoulders to look at the world boldly,
I see talent coldly
Damning me to stooped attrition.
Mine was a beggar's mission.
To dreams of beauty I should have been born blind.

I should have been content to walk behind,
Watching the mirror-stones
For the reflection of God's delight:
A second-hand teller of the story,
A second-hand glory.
It was not right
That my mind should have echoed life's overtones,
That I should have seen a flower
Petalled in mighty power.

Plough-horses

Their glossy flanks and manes outshone
The flying splinters of the sun.

The tranquil rhythm of that team
Was as slow-flowing meadow stream.

And I saw Phidias' chisel there –
An ocean stallion, mountain mare,

Seeing, with eyes the Spirit unsealed,
Plough-horses in a quiet field.

Snail

I go from you, I recede,
Not by steps violent,
But as a snail backing
From the lewd finger of humanity.

I go from you as a snail
Into my twisted habitation.

And you!
It does not matter how you
React. I know the shadow-ways
Of Self.
I know the last sharp bend
And the volleyed light.

You are lost.
You can merely chase the silver I have let
Fall from my purse.
You follow silver
And not follow me.

The Weary Horse

The weary horse on which I ride
Is language vitiate
That cannot take in its stride
Bank, stream and gate.

Its eyes have the blank look
Of a memoried fool,
Or a Victorian book
In a modern school.

Pygmalion

I saw her in a field, a stone-proud woman
Hugging the monster Passion's granite child,
Engirdled by the ditches of Roscommon,
Stone ditches round her waist like serpents coiled.
Her lips were frozen in the signature
Of Lust, her hair was set eternally,
No Grecian goddess, for her face was poor,
A twisted face, like Hardship's face, to me.
And who she was I queried every man
From Ballaghaderreen to grassy Boyle,
And all replied: a stone Pygmalion
Once lifted to a grey terrific smile.
I said: At dawn tomorrow she will be
Clay-sensuous. But they only smiled at me.

1939–46

Anna Quinn

O God above,
Must I forever be a dream of love?
Must I forever see as in a glass
The loveliness of life before me pass,
Like Anna Quinn or sunlight on the grass?

Primrose

Upon a bank I sat, a child made seer
Of one small primrose flowering in my mind.
Better than wealth it is, said I, to find
One small page of Truth's manuscript made clear.
I looked at Christ transfigured without fear –
The light was very beautiful and kind,
And where the Holy Ghost in flame had signed
I read it through the lenses of a tear.
And then my sight grew dim, I could not see
The primrose that had lighted me to Heaven,
And there was but the shadow of a tree
Ghostly among the stars. The years that pass
Like tired soldiers nevermore have given
Moments to see wonders in the grass.

Memory of My Father

Every old man I see
Reminds me of my father
When he had fallen in love with death
One time when sheaves were gathered.

That man I saw in Gardiner Street
Stumble on the kerb was one,
He stared at me half-eyed,
I might have been his son.

And I remember the musician
Faltering over his fiddle
In Bayswater, London,
He too set me the riddle.

Every old man I see
In October-coloured weather
Seems to say to me:
'I was once your father.'

Christmas, 1939

O Divine Baby in the cradle,
All that is poet in me
Is the dream I dreamed of Your Childhood
And the dream You dreamed of me.

O Divine Baby in the cradle,
All that is truth in me
Is my mind tuned to the cadence
Of a child's philosophy.

O Divine Baby in the cradle,
All that is pride in me
Is my mind bowed in homage
Upon Your Mother's knee.

O Divine Baby in the cradle,
All that is joy in me
Is that I have saved from the ruin
Of my soul Your Infancy.

Christmas Eve Remembered

I see them going to the chapel
To confess their sins. Christmas Eve
In a parish in Monaghan.
Poor parish! and yet memory does weave
For me about those folk
A romantic cloak.

No snow, but in their minds
The fields and roads are white;
They may be talking of the turkey markets
Or foreign politics, but to-night
Their plain, hard country words
Are Christ's singing birds.

Bicycles scoot by. Old women
Cling to the grass margin:
Their thoughts are earthy, but their minds move
In dreams of the Blessed Virgin,
For One in Bethlehem
Has kept their dreams safe for them.

'Did you hear from Tom this Christmas?'
'These are the dark days.'
'Maguire's shop did a great trade,
Turnover double – so Maguire says.'
'I can't delay now, Jem,
Lest I be late in Bethlehem.'

Like this my memory saw,
Like this my childhood heard
These pilgrims of the North . . .
And memory you have me spared
A light to follow them
Who go to Bethlehem.

To the Man After the Harrow

Now leave the check-reins slack,
The seed is flying far today –
The seed like stars against the black
Eternity of April clay.

This seed is potent as the seed
Of knowledge in the Hebrew Book,
So drive your horses in the creed
Of God the Father as a stook.

Forget the men on Brady's hill.
Forget what Brady's boy may say,
For destiny will not fulfil
Unless you let the harrow play.

Forget the worm's opinion too
Of hooves and pointed harrow-pins,
For you are driving your horses through
The mist where Genesis begins.

Spraying the Potatoes

The barrels of blue potato-spray
Stood on a headland of July
Beside an orchard wall where roses
Were young girls hanging from the sky.

The flocks of green potato-stalks
Were blossom spread for sudden flight,
The Kerr's Pinks in a frivelled blue,
The Arran Banners wearing white.

And over that potato-field
A lazy veil of woven sun.
Dandelions growing on headlands, showing
Their unloved hearts to everyone.

And I was there with the knapsack sprayer
On the barrel's edge poised. A wasp was floating
Dead on a sunken briar leaf
Over a copper-poisoned ocean.

The axle-roll of a rut-locked cart
Broke the burnt stick of noon in two.
An old man came through a corn-field
Remembering his youth and some Ruth he knew.

He turned my way. 'God further the work.'
He echoed an ancient farming prayer.
I thanked him. He eyed the potato-drills.
He said: 'You are bound to have good ones there.'

We talked and our talk was a theme of kings,
A theme for strings. He hunkered down
In the shade of the orchard wall. O roses,
The old man dies in the young girl's frown.

And poet lost to potato-fields,
Remembering the lime and copper smell
Of the spraying barrels he is not lost
Or till blossomed stalks cannot weave a spell.

Pilgrims

I saw them kneeling by the holy well –
It was for life, life, life they prayed:
Life that for a farmer is land enough to keep two horses,
Life that is a healthy husband to a maid.

I saw them climbing the holy mountain –
It was the knowledge, knowledge, knowledge of life they pursued:
Knowledge that is in knowing what fair to sell the cattle in,
Knowledge that is in being able to cart an acre from a field.

I saw them lying on the burning stones –
It was vision, vision, vision they desired:
Vision that is forecasting a mare's hour of foaling,
Vision that is catching the idler, newly hired.

I saw them kneeling, climbing and prostrate –
It was love, love, love they found:
Love that is Christ green walking from the summer headlands
To His scarecrow cross in the turnip-ground.

Stony Grey Soil

O stony grey soil of Monaghan,
The laugh from my love you thieved;
You took the gay child of my passion
And gave me your clod-conceived.

You clogged the feet of my boyhood,
And I believed that my stumble
Had the poise and stride of Apollo
And his voice my thick-tongued mumble.

You told me the plough was immortal!
O green-life-conquering plough!
Your mandril strained, your coulter blunted
In the smooth lea-field of my brow.

You sang on steaming dunghills
A song of cowards' brood,
You perfumed my clothes with weasel itch,
You fed me on swinish food.

You flung a ditch on my vision
Of beauty, love and truth.
O stony grey soil of Monaghan,
You burgled my bank of youth!

Lost the long hours of pleasure,
All the women that love young men.
O can I still stroke the monster's back
Or write with unpoisoned pen

His name in these lonely verses,
Or mention the dark fields where
The first gay flight of my lyric
Got caught in a peasant's prayer.

Mullahinsha, Drummeril, Black Shanco –
Wherever I turn I see
In the stony grey soil of Monaghan
Dead loves that were born for me.

A Christmas Childhood

I

One side of the potato-pits was white with frost –
How wonderful that was, how wonderful!
And when we put our ears to the paling-post
The music that came out was magical.

The light between the ricks of hay and straw
Was a hole in Heaven's gable. An apple tree
With its December-glinting fruit we saw –
O you, Eve, were the world that tempted me

To eat the knowledge that grew in clay
And death the germ within it! Now and then
I can remember something of the gay
Garden that was childhood's. Again

The tracks of cattle to a drinking-place,
A green stone lying sideways in a ditch,
Or any common sight, the transfigured face
Of a beauty that the world did not touch.

II

My father played the melodion
Outside at our gate;
There were stars in the morning east
And they danced to his music.

Across the wild bogs his melodion called
To Lennons and Callans.
As I pulled on my trousers in a hurry
I knew some strange thing had happened.

Outside in the cow-house my mother
Made the music of milking;
The light of her stable-lamp was a star
And the frost of Bethlehem made it twinkle.

A water-hen screeched in the bog,
Mass-going feet
Crunched the wafer-ice on the pot-holes,
Somebody wistfully twisted the bellows wheel.

My child poet picked out the letters
On the grey stone,
In silver the wonder of a Christmas townland,
The winking glitter of a frosty dawn.

Cassiopeia was over
Cassidy's hanging hill,
I looked and three whin bushes rode across
The horizon – the Three Wise Kings.

An old man passing said:
'Can't he make it talk –
The melodion.' I hid in the doorway
And tightened the belt of my box-pleated coat.

I nicked six nicks on the door-post
With my penknife's big blade –
There was a little one for cutting tobacco.
And I was six Christmases of age.

My father played the melodion,
My mother milked the cows,
And I had a prayer like a white rose pinned
On the Virgin Mary's blouse.

Art McCooey

I recover now the time I drove
Cart-loads of dung to an outlying farm –
My foreign possessions in Shancoduff –
With the enthusiasm of a man who sees life simply.

The steam rising from the load is still
Warm enough to thaw my frosty fingers.
In Donnybrook in Dublin ten years later
I see that empire now and the empire builder.

Sometimes meeting a neighbour
In country love-enchantment,
The old mare pulls over to the bank and leaves us
To fiddle folly where November dances.

We wove our disappointments and successes
To patterns of a town-bred logic:
'She might have been sick . . .' 'No, never before,
A mystery, Pat, and they all appear so modest.'

We exchanged our fool advices back and forth:
'It easily could be their cow was calving,
And sure the rain was desperate that night . . .'
Somewhere in the mists a light was laughing.

We played with the frilly edges of reality
While we puffed our cigarettes;
And sometimes Owney Martin's splitting yell
Would knife the dreamer that the land begets.

'I'll see you after Second Mass on Sunday.'
'Right-o, right-o.' The mare moves on again.
A wheel rides over a heap of gravel
And the mare goes skew-ways like a blinded hen.

Down the lane-way of the popular banshees
By Paddy Bradley's; mud to the ankles;
A hare is grazing in Mat Rooney's meadow;
Maggie Byrne is prowling for dead branches.

Ten loads before tea-time. Was that the laughter
Of the evening bursting school?
The sun sinks low and large behind the hills of Cavan,
A stormy-looking sunset. 'Brave and cool.'

Wash out the cart with a bucket of water and a wangel
Of wheaten straw. Jupiter looks down.
Unlearnedly and unreasonably poetry is shaped,
Awkwardly but alive in the unmeasured womb.

The Long Garden

It was the garden of the golden apples,
A long garden between a railway and a road,
In the sow's rooting where the hen scratches
We dipped our fingers in the pockets of God.

In the thistly hedge old boots were flying sandals
By which we travelled through the childhood skies,
Old buckets rusty-holed with half-hung handles
Were drums to play when old men married wives.

The pole that lifted the clothes-line in the middle
Was the flag-pole on a prince's palace when
We looked at it through fingers crossed to riddle
In evening sunlight miracles for men.

It was the garden of the golden apples,
And when the Carrick train went by we knew
That we could never die till something happened,
Like wishing for a fruit that never grew,

Or wanting to be up on Candlefort
Above the village with its shops and mill.
The racing cyclists' gasp-gapped reports
Hinted of pubs where life can drink his fill.

And when the sun went down into Drumcatton
And the New Moon by its little finger swung
From the telegraph wires, we knew how God had happened
And what the blackbird in the whitethorn sang.

It was the garden of the golden apples,
The half-way house where we had stopped a day
Before we took the west road to Drumcatton
Where the sun was always setting on the play.

Why Sorrow?

[A fragment]

It was the month of May. Father Mat walked among
His cows that evening, dreaming of a song
That Christ had closed the window on.
                              Now the priest's pride
Was a Roman poet's hearing of the Crucified:
Apollo's unbaptized pagan who can show
To simple eyes what Christians never know –
Was it the unspeakable beauty of hell?
The priest looked once – twice – and fell.

The bleeding body of sorrow, no pattern
Woven, the excitement of a child
That remembers the ditches where dead leaves have rotted,
A suddenness of green and light,
And the balls of mud that were spun to spheres
Within the orbit of the road-roller's wheels:
All that was true before the piteous death of the Cross.
No earth-love was transfigured on that Hill,
All flattened out, most prostrate, muddy-mouthed.

The priest moved on. He swung
His blackthorn at a pebble of the sun.
He saw the daisies now and the white
Confirmation dresses of the alder trees,
And he heard the people passing, laughing –
                                        'I might
Have eaten like these
Life's leavened bread that has mysteries
Marvellous as the wafer consecrated
Each morning with words that are blots in the book of my fate.'

But his people needed him,
His people needed him,
His people needed him.

He was the sledge that smashed the dark resistance
Of time for those who never could fly;
He was the people's need where the little fields
Of Cavan gagged the mouth of prophecy.

His pride lay between the hammer and the thing
That he was striking at. Every blow
Squashed flat something that knew of beauty,
Drove joy into a wet, weedy onion-row.

But his people needed him,
Needed him,
Needed him.

His cows were heavy with calf. He liked to talk
Of things growing and growthy till the people thought
Him the old-time priest who took life as it came,
Looked into the hearts of his people, covered their shame
With the white cloak of Grace, attended the sick,
Gave Christ, and then talked with Paddy and Mick
Of the work of the seasons: 'Your potatoes are doing
Better than my own . . .'
'Tis the farmyard manuring.'

He was a part of the place, as natural as
The stones in grazing fields that are not seen
By those who walk the ridges. Yet he was all
That the servant of the Lord needed to be,
A mud-walled house that was Truth's citadel.

The children of Dromore looked up at him
Trustingly, hero-worshippingly. His humilities
Were of a high angel that stooped and caressed
The sinful heads of poor children. That man was blessed
Above all other priests that they had known,
A soul with no sharp edges – a simple one.
His farmer face, soft eyes, white hair,
His slow flat tread, his thick tongue for bargaining fair
Or for prayer.

His father was a farmer in Corofin.
He had six fields with soil like soap,
Where rushes grew and grasses like steel wires,
Blue in the sunshine. Down the shivering slope

Water ran in sheets of winter.
And out of this sour soil he squeezed
The answer to his wife's wishes;
In steely grass and green rushes
Was woven the vestments of a priest.

The eldest daughter rose to be
A teacher in a school.
Mat was the youngest. Father took
His rosary and at a stool
Knelt and prayed for something special,
Something that was never mentioned.
And the fire went out behind their heels,
And Mat grew up like July in the fields.

And as he grew they prayed that he was growing
A priest. He was soft and easy-going;
No wild singing in the evening lanes
Or at the night cross-roads. But through the dusk window-panes
Looking out where ducks were coming gabbling in
From the frog-croaking bogs of Corofin,
A calf sucking the edge of a tub,
The Evening Star musing in the East,
Behind the house the giggle of girls.
                         He was a priest
Already – he only had to grow;
The flower was in the seed.
Twin flowers, perhaps – he sometimes saw
The magic worlds of another law.

It was the Garden of the Golden Apples,
A long garden between a railway and a road,
In the sow's rooting where the hen scratches
He dipped his fingers in the pocket of a rich god.

In the thistly hedge old boots were flying sandals
By which he travelled through the childhood skies,
Old buckets rusty-holed with half-hung handles
Were drums to beat when old men married wives.

The pole that lifted the clothes-line in the middle
Was the flag-pole on a prince's palace when
He looked at it through fingers crossed to riddle
In evening sunlight miracles for men.

It was the Garden of the Golden Apples,
And when the Carrick train went by he knew
That he could never die till something happened,
Like wishing for a fruit that never grew,

Or wanting to be up on Candlefort
Above the village with its shops and mill.
The racing cyclists' gasp-gapped reports
Hinted of pubs where love can drink his fill.

And when the sun went down into Drumcatton
And the new moon by her little finger swung
From the telegraph wires, he knew how life had happened
And what the blackbird in the whitethorn sang.

It was the Garden of the Golden Apples,
The half-way house where he had stopped a day
Before he took the west road to Drumcatton
Where the sun was always setting on the play.

And when the years brought loving on,
He was deep in love with one –
Mary, Queen of Heaven.

She was every girl he knew,
Nimble-footed, daring too.

She was laughter on the stiles
In the evenings of July
When the lads were playing skittles
On the dusty road. Her cry,

'Good man, Mat'. She could run
The hundred yards with any one.
And she could sling a stone above
McCabe's tall poplar. Love, ah love!

All that was flesh of womankind
Was the Virgin Mary in his mind.
And lonely as a lover then,
Separate in a world of men,
He walked and wondered why
He could not reach the gaiety.
The gap was bushed and Christ was always
Like an old farmer guarding it
From neighbouring trespass.
He was a grey, stooped old man of Cavan,
Christ herding a ragged cow in a patch of dry grass.

Every penny that the school-teacher earned,
Save fifteen shillings weekly for her keep,
She posted home. And Mat went to college
And all things turned out as they had prayed.
This done,
At thirty-eight herself became a nun.

Through the cool meadows that lay along the river
And through the flaggered swamp the priest went on;
On the back of his neck there burned a disc of sun.
                          Was this the river Styx
And that man in shirt-sleeves with a shovel, Charon,
Or only Michael McCabe? – he who rowed sorrow over
To bluebell beauty on the wild hills of Seola,
Those hills that were always swinging their beauty in –
Original Sin –

Oh the screaming children on the greening ridges.
The trees that were before the Cross was sawn
Were worthy to be worshipped. Come draw your wages
In evening silver, in pure gold at dawn.

Father Mat looked down at a coltsfoot blossom
And loved it more than ever he loved the Sacrament –
And here was the symbol of an old joy.
Success – the earth cheers Christ human, not divine.

The May Devotions in the chapel stirred
His imagination which, poised like a bird
Over a turnip field in a June sky,
Picked out the coloured leaves in memory.

       In the dim chapel was the grey
Mumble of prayer
To the Queen of May,
The Virgin Mary with her school-girl air.

The priest was seeing her, a girl
Of fifteen. She sits and listens to
The wandering poet who has come (indeed!)
To talk with her mother of times they both knew.

He sits one side of the fire dandling the tongs,
The mother the other side, Mary by the dresser.
The tea is made and as they drink the mother
Marvels at the scholar,
His indifference to girls and dancing and the world's bother.

The mother goes out to milk the cows. Says he:
'How many miles to Babylon? With me
Beside you it is just to dream . . .'
The childhood of the priest cried out: 'Beware
Of the evil spell in all poetry.'
       And he was saying a prayer
In the dim chapel all the while,
But the Gospel was printed over an older writing
And its damnation was crawling under the Host.

O despair! O despair! O despair!
My people want and I must be
For them
Their final surety.
I doubt
But must not let them see
That I am signing with a lie
Their cheques of holy constancy.
O Truth, I
This evening ask
How I may
Sieve me salvation
In the riddle of clay,
And from Morning's temptation
To dally with day
Keep me I pray.

. . . *

'I vexed my father until he swore
And beat my mother till she screamed (for more)' –
Father Mat listened with bowed head
As the earth came in to be burned, every stalk
That grew green in the heart to be uprooted,
Every memory that surprised with an unChristly pleasure,
The clod growing a daisy, the oily black stones in the river,
Put away for ever.
                    All that was
His heart when he was happy must not be;
The Way of Christ's Sorrow is shaded by no tree.

His human lips talked on:
'My son,
The poor in spirit only shall wear the crown.
The down
Shall creep in the low door
To Heaven's floor.'

All poetry in nature or in book
Must be outcast this night. We must not look
Behind us at the pitiful beauty of those
That lost the war, but kept their magic power.
O the wild, fearful happiness of the poet
Is almost too great a load for Christ's shoulders.

A little girl came, and whisperingly
Said: 'Father, I'm a child of Mary.'
She told him how she once had loved the pianist
Who taught the convent girls. One day
He came to her father's house to hear her play.

* 4 pages missing here.

He said her fingers on the keys were the hopping feet of hungry
    birds.
He told her of a strange world. And then?
He gave her loneliness for ever.
She knew nothing about the ways of men
Until that day. 'O Father, heed my sorrow.'

The Confessor sighed and thought: Who seizes a star
Breaks the balance of justice. Mercies are
A cone of loose rubble piled upon the Moon –
'My daughter you are the mystery in the piano's tune.'

As Father Mat walked home
Venus was in the Western sky
And through her broken maidenhead
He saw the womb of poetry.

The children dancing in the dusk
Cried with voices of surprise
That were never twice repeated:
'God the Gay is not the Wise.'

'Take your choice, take your choice',
Called the breeze through the bridge's eye:
'The domestic Virgin and Her Child,
Or Venus with her ecstasy.'

To the lives of the Saints he turned,
To Saint John of the Cross and Teresa of Avila,
And all the chapters shouted, 'Jesus, Jesus,
The Defeated One, is He whom we must follow.'

Through his parlour window down the old yew path
A vista opened and a rhododendron
Swung sideways like a dancing girl and winked
Temptation to his heart, the dim temptation
Of middle-age.

A death-bed call today, yet even death
Up that long lane in a pocket of the hills
Was not the Cross of Christ; the old romantic
Was greeting death as merrily as a wedding feast.
Within the house he knew every rag and stick,
The mean unmade bed behind the kitchen,
The sights they hurried to hide when he came in.
His soft eyes pierced
Into the secret rooms of their homes and hearts
Where everything was topsy-turvy: an unwashed shirt
Kicked under the bed, and the chamber-pot
That the woman forgot to empty,
A stolen pitch-fork standing in a corner.
And the old man in bed, his beads in his fingers
Counting old sins.
Death was as easy as harvest in Seola.

His hand upon the dash-board of a cart,
Father Mat was standing
Talking to Michael Duffy about fairs,
The price of pigs and store-cattle –
Like a dealer in the Shercock fair bawling in the doorways of shops.
His heavy hat was square upon his head
Like a Christian Brother's,
His eyes were watery like an old man's eyes,
And out of his flat nose grew spiky hairs.
Michael Duffy wondered as he saw him thus:
So like mere earth and yet not one of us.

It was the gap
Between the seasons, and the days moved slowly,
With labouring men sleeping on headlands among the nettles
And long arms hooked over gates that brightened
The gravel patches on the June road.
The priest spoke wistfully, rurally, heavily,
And no one could know that he was seeing
Down the shaft of the gate's light, horses growing wings;
The midges caught in the searchlight
Were beautiful, unChristian things.

His curate cycled by – to the Village Hall,
He had the haughty intellectual look
Of the man who never reads in brook or book,
The man who has not climbed and cannot fall.
Father Ned was fair
And freckled just the slightest bit. He was sharp,
A diligent priest who never slurred a word
Of Mass or litany; a man who was never late
For train or chapel. He had the sins
Of men card-indexed – fixed in permanent values:
He could tell the mortal ones at a mile's distance in all their
    several grins.
Each day he smoked five cigarettes
And never six. He could speak to Christ
As to his brother the publican of Cootehill.
The Parish Priest was afraid:
There was a man
Who'd write and tell the Bishop tales of scandal,
Or of how he, Father Mat, talked to himself
And worshipped more the flowers in the garden
Than God. But Ned was scarce of understanding
Everything that Maynooth had put no mark on.
Ned was the works that kept the parish going:

The dance-hall, the new decorations in the chapel.
But the people were shy of him, from him they ran
To Father Mat, who was both priest and man.

Again that unholy beauty struck his eyes
And Christ, the Coward of Gethsemane,
Cried out: 'Father, Father . . .'
The dancer that danced
In the hearts of men:
'Look! I have shown it to you before,
The bogs, the grey hills, the dirty rags
Of living excited
That no man has seen and died.
            I broke away
And rule all the dominions that are rare;
I took with me all the answers to every prayer
That young men and girls pray. Love, happiness, riches,
Christ cannot give. He is the bitter-tasted, wrong-turned.
You will get
From Christ if you pray for love a laugh too late,
And riches Christly-come will be desire
Without escape for it.'

The sun crept round
And June was a hum over dusty ground.
Confirmation Day,
The Bishop of the Diocese came that way.
He chrismed the children and slapped their humble cheeks
In token of the descending Paraclete –
Be wife, be wife, be spread –
The Holy Spirit consummates.
He spoke, the Bishop spoke, of Father Mat,
In him the people of that parish had

A priest who went the good old ways and asked
No questions. Doing his job in simpleness.
'You plough, you sow, you reap, you buy and sell
And sing and eat and sleep. All this is well done
In the Name of the Holy One.'

Father Mat laughed with the mothers of the children
Who smiled, acknowledging their approval of
The Bishop's words – they seconded the motion.
And as the Bishop passed down the centre aisle,
Blessing to right and left, 'twas Father Mat
Their eyes were fixed on. A proud people,
Proud of a parish priest whose words begat
Odd music in the silences.
               Of his own Confirmation Day
Father Mat was thinking – when he first found in clay
The secret of a different Deity written . . .
Before the sun went down into Drumcatton.

O Fear,
When consciousness blows through the debris
We are unhomed. Truth's insanity
Is a spell that men must hold to; when they wake
Not even dust is left for all their striving.

So one dull day he knelt and struck his breast
And denied the sun and the earth. And Jesus Christ
Turned him round in his path.

Everywhere he went now grief was come or arriving.
In Casey's house where merriment had been
Longer than scandalous gossip could recall,
Where they had drunk long and loved long
When the factory men love-seeking left their towns.

Lilacs grew before that door and roses
More prosperous than roses anywhere,
Forget-me-nots in rings – not marriage rings –
A cherry tree that swung a welcoming gate.

And you could hear,
On summer evenings coming from the village,
Loud laughter from the kitchen of the silly
Girls that were bastardy's delight –
Their screams were larks by day and nightingales by night.

The mothers – there were four – had never learned
To look outside the door when footsteps passed;
They did not heed what talkers talking much
Said about them as they went to Sunday Mass.

Away back, Octobers lamp-lit that house of pleasure
And memory many-windowed; each one showed
A new crop of lovers gathered in the kitchen,
An old crop blowing down the sleety road.

All within that house had learned of the earth
How to be quick like a season to grow and blossom,
How to be without remorse when the windy weather
Takes down the leaves. Old lovers dream with Autumn.

The old priest crossed that threshold with the pity
Of Christ. And what life taught of take and spend
Was forgotten, and four generations wept in a squalid corner
For tomorrows that would tell the shame of them.

Why should this be?
O ease, O rest,
There are wool-packs in the west.
Rain fills the evening. At the sharp bend of the Seola road

The whitethorns are drenched,
The dripping branches on the carts going home
Is a holy-water blessing this hour.
But this that was once a miracle is now
To Father Mat the abominable symbol of
The Golden Calf.
The rattle of buckets, rolling of barrels under
Down-spouts, the leading-in of foals
Were happenings dipped deep in pagan wonder,
Springs of life.

     He cast his soul's
Pride in the ditch and he was wearing
The charity-stained dress of grief.
The rain-lighted lanes of Seola were graveyards feeding
But in sorrow was the mystery of being.

One day he said: 'I shall not rove
Out of this miserable groove.'
Contrition. He confessed his sins
To his own curate, Father Ned.
And though 'twas degradation that
He saw when he had bowed his head,
He held to the belittlement
– Through the floor my soul. The Lord's
Tabernacle is underneath the flooring-boards.

Now he was with his people, one of them.
What they saw, he saw too,
And nothing more; what they looked at,
And what to them was true, was true
For him. He was in the crowd,
A nobody who had been proud.

From the level of the people he could see
No hills beyond new-green, no raw flesh bleeding,
No light astonishing as a knife drawn
In Shercock cattle-fair at dawn.
The crowd is mud, mud to the knees,
And Pride you were a star-high stand,
Yet maybe I'll find in Charity's
Illiterate book of pieties
Apollo's writing in a Christian hand.

He went to Lough Derg, Saint Patrick's Purgatory,
Father Mat went to the Island of the poor,
Where every leaf that is green is changed to fire
And everything that makes art and literature
Is a thing to be abhorred – impure desire.

On bare knees they prayed around the rings
Of stones that once were holy walls that bound
The flood of human desire
Into a turbine that spun Time's mill-wheels round.
They were monks then with wants – like women
Or flowers in winter – stretched on their backs
To ease their too strong loving . . .
                    But today here were lacks,
Anaemic hearts that said to life: 'Stay out',
Life that was not coming in. Shopkeepers strolled about.
Then a young man painted his shadow on
Saint Brigid's ring of penitential stone.
His back was to the sun though he was praying
For what the sun has thrown to fools all time.

He was a clerk from Dublin, unemployed,
Twenty-seven years old. He was in love
With a waitress in the city.

'O God, give me a job and I will prove
My faith and come each year. She is pretty.
Once when my passion broke
The thin banks of youth, she held my wrists
And smiled away my shame as a joke.
There's a job in Thomas Street; I'm on their lists;
But the lists are long as roads that Hope is walking.
That shape at the rise, I know, is no house of rest
But the mist
Risen from tears that were wept at many a mocking . . .'

Father Mat was tempted: Is the way of living
That you are praying for in this God's giving?
Ah lad, upon the road of life
'Tis best to dance with Chance's wife
And let the road-menders that follow
Sweep remorse into a hollow.

A girl went round the holy stones,
About thirty-five she was with a long nose.
Was she too praying for what she
Herself was saying, 'Keep from me'?
Father Mat had seen her before –
The extra woman on the kitchen floor.
She had one chance.

'But no one ever came again
To ask why I was born a woman.
No one was ever man, but only men,
Only crowds and never the companion.
I had to search, I had to be brave –
And bravery is piteous in a maid.
I danced, I danced
With dancing clowns,

I smiled and planned –
I went to towns and walked main streets and fair green
And saw no man but only men
Shouting the price of pigs and cows
Or quarrelling in a public house.
O the search that we know is vain!'

Day, night, vigil, dawn –
The Pilgrimage went on,
The sun came up over Donegal
And jeered at what was pitiful.

Over cups of black tea they laughed,
Shortening the day that was a measureless day
Of Purgatory. Women, their bare legs asplay,
Lay on their backs upon the rise where grew green grass –
They were emptied out waiting for love that never was
A wink of the sun.
It was like a day by the sea.
New pilgrims came and yesterday's paper
Passed across panting bellies, fluttering
Hands reached to catch the stale news of war.
What earth toy were earth's men fighting for?

Far away beyond the water
The miles that are not miles
But ideas of death.

An old man pointed a finger to his face
Where was a cancerous hole:
'Was God not good to me?' he said
As he moved back the pad of cotton wool.
'That happened coming from Mass,
An accident, a fall upon stone it was.

But it will kill me painlessly, for I
Have asked this at Saint Patrick's Purgatory.'
'O God is good', the listeners said.
The Cynic whispered to Father Mat . . .

The Great Hunger

I

Clay is the word and clay is the flesh
Where the potato-gatherers like mechanized scare-crows move
Along the side-fall of the hill – Maguire and his men.
If we watch them an hour is there anything we can prove
Of life as it is broken-backed over the Book
Of Death? Here crows gabble over worms and frogs
And the gulls like old newspapers are blown clear of the hedges,
   luckily.
Is there some light of imagination in these wet clods?
Or why do we stand here shivering?
                              Which of these men
Loved the light and the queen
Too long virgin? Yesterday was summer. Who was it promised
   marriage to himself
Before apples were hung from the ceilings for Hallowe'en?
We will wait and watch the tragedy to the last curtain,
Till the last soul passively like a bag of wet clay
Rolls down the side of the hill, diverted by the angles
Where the plough missed or a spade stands, straitening the way.

A dog lying on a torn jacket under a heeled-up cart,
A horse nosing along the posied headland, trailing
A rusty plough. Three heads hanging between wide-apart
Legs. October playing a symphony on a slack wire paling.
Maguire watches the drills flattened out
And the flints that lit a candle for him on a June altar
Flameless. The drills slipped by and the days slipped by
And he trembled his head away and ran free from the world's
    halter,
And thought himself wiser than any man in the townland
When he laughed over pints of porter
Of how he came free from every net spread
In the gaps of experience. He shook a knowing head
And pretended to his soul
That children are tedious in hurrying fields of April
Where men are spanging across wide furrows,
Lost in the passion that never needs a wife –
The pricks that pricked were the pointed pins of harrows.
Children scream so loud that the crows could bring
The seed of an acre away with crow-rude jeers.
Patrick Maguire, he called his dog and he flung a stone in the
    air
And hallooed the birds away that were the birds of the years.
Turn over the weedy clods and tease out the tangled skeins.
What is he looking for there?
He thinks it is a potato, but we know better
Than his mud-gloved fingers probe in this insensitive hair.

'Move forward the basket and balance it steady
In this hollow. Pull down the shafts of that cart, Joe,
And straddle the horse,' Maguire calls.
'The wind's over Brannagan's, now that means rain.
Graip up some withered stalks and see that no potato falls
Over the tail-board going down the ruckety pass –

And *that's* a job we'll have to do in December,
Gravel it and build a kerb on the bog-side. Is that Cassidy's ass
Out in my clover? Curse o' God –
Where is that dog?
Never where he's wanted.' Maguire grunts and spits
Through a clay-wattled moustache and stares about him from the
    height.
His dream changes again like the cloud-swung wind
And he is not so sure now if his mother was right
When she praised the man who made a field his bride.

Watch him, watch him, that man on a hill whose spirit
Is a wet sack flapping about the knees of time.
He lives that his little fields may stay fertile when his own body
Is spread in the bottom of a ditch under two coulters crossed in
    Christ's Name.

He was suspicious in his youth as a rat near strange bread
When girls laughed; when they screamed he knew that meant
The cry of fillies in season. He could not walk
The easy road to his destiny. He dreamt
The innocence of young brambles to hooked treachery.
O the grip, O the grip of irregular fields! No man escapes.
It could not be that back of the hills love was free
And ditches straight.
No monster hand lifted up children and put down apes
As here.
                  'O God if I had been wiser!'
That was his sigh like the brown breeze in the thistles.
He looks towards his house and haggard. 'O God if I had been
    wiser!'
But now a crumpled leaf from the whitethorn bushes
Darts like a frightened robin, and the fence
Shows the green of after-grass through a little window,

And he knows that his own heart is calling his mother a liar.
God's truth is life – even the grotesque shapes of its foulest fire.

The horse lifts its head and cranes
Through the whins and stones
To lip late passion in the crawling clover.
In the gap there's a bush weighted with boulders like morality,
The fools of life bleed if they climb over.

The wind leans from Brady's, and the coltsfoot leaves are holed
    with rust,
Rain fills the cart-tracks and the sole-plate grooves;
A yellow sun reflects in Donaghmoyne
The poignant light in puddles shaped by hooves.

Come with me, Imagination, into this iron house
And we will watch from the doorway the years run back,
And we will know what a peasant's left hand wrote on the page.
Be easy, October. No cackle hen, horse neigh, tree sough, duck
    quack.

II

Maguire was faithful to death:
He stayed with his mother till she died
At the age of ninety-one.
She stayed too long,
Wife and mother in one.
When she died
The knuckle-bones were cutting the skin of her son's backside
And he was sixty-five.

O he loved his mother
Above all others.

O he loved his ploughs
And he loved his cows
And his happiest dream
Was to clean his arse
With perennial grass
On the bank of some summer stream;
To smoke his pipe
In a sheltered gripe
In the middle of July –
His face in a mist
And two stones in his fist
And an impotent worm on his thigh.

But his passion became a plague
For he grew feeble bringing the vague
Women of his mind to lust nearness,
Once a week at least flesh must make an appearance.

So Maguire got tired
Of the no-target gun fired
And returned to his headlands of carrots and cabbage,
To the fields once again
Where eunuchs can be men
And life is more lousy than savage.

III

Poor Paddy Maguire, a fourteen-hour day
He worked for years. It was he that lit the fire
And boiled the kettle and gave the cows their hay.
His mother, tall, hard as a Protestant spire,
Came down the stairs bare-foot at the kettle-call
And talked to her son sharply: 'Did you let
The hens out, you?' She had a venomous drawl

And a wizened face like moth-eaten leatherette.
Two black cats peeped between the banisters
And gloated over the bacon-fizzling pan.
Outside the window showed tin canisters.
The snipe of Dawn fell like a whirring stone
And Patrick on a headland stood alone.

The pull is on the traces; it is March
And a cold old black wind is blowing from Dundalk.
The twisting sod rolls over on her back –
The virgin screams before the irresistible sock.
No worry on Maguire's mind this day
Except that he forgot to bring his matches.
'Hop back there, Polly, hoy back, woa, wae.'
From every second hill a neighbour watches
With all the sharpened interest of rivalry.
Yet sometimes when the sun comes through a gap
These men know God the Father in a tree:
The Holy Spirit is the rising sap,
And Christ will be the green leaves that will come
At Easter from the sealed and guarded tomb.

Primroses and the unearthly start of ferns
Among the blackthorn shadows in the ditch,
A dead sparrow and an old waistcoat. Maguire learns
As the horses turn slowly round the which is which
Of love and fear and things half born to mind.
He stands between the plough-handles and he sees
At the end of a long furrow his name signed
Among the poets, prostitutes. With all miseries
He is one. Here with the unfortunate
Who for half moments of paradise
Pay out good days and wait and wait
For sunlight-woven cloaks. O to be wise

As Respectability that knows the price of all things
And marks God's truth in pounds and pence and farthings.

IV

April, and no one able to calculate
How far is it to harvest. They put down
The seeds blindly with sensuous groping fingers,
And sensual sleep dreams subtly underground.
Tomorrow is Wednesday – who cares?
'Remember Eileen Farrelly? I was thinking
A man might do a damned sight worse . . .' That voice is blown
Through a hole in a garden wall –
And who was Eileen now cannot be known.

The cattle are out on grass,
The corn is coming up evenly.
The farm folk are hurrying to catch Mass:
Christ will meet them at the end of the world, the slow and
      speedier.
But the fields say: only Time can bless.

Maguire knelt beside a pillar where he could spit
Without being seen. He turned an old prayer round:
'Jesus, Mary and Joseph pray for us
Now and at the Hour.' Heaven dazzled death.
'Wonder should I cross-plough that turnip-ground.'
The tension broke. The congregation lifted its head
As one man and coughed in unison.
Five hundred hearts were hungry for life –
Who lives in Christ shall never die the death.
And the candle-lit Altar and the flowers
And the pregnant Tabernacle lifted a moment to Prophecy
Out of the clayey hours.

Maguire sprinkled his face with holy water
As the congregation stood up for the Last Gospel.
He rubbed the dust off his knees with his palm, and then
Coughed the prayer phlegm up from his throat and sighed: Amen.

Once one day in June when he was walking
Among his cattle in the Yellow Meadow
He met a girl carrying a basket –
And he was then a young and heated fellow.
Too earnest, too earnest! He rushed beyond the thing
To the unreal. And he saw Sin
Written in letters larger than John Bunyan dreamt of.
For the strangled impulse there is no redemption.
And that girl was gone and he was counting
The dangers in the fields where love ranted.
He was helpless. He saw his cattle
And stroked their flanks in lieu of wife to handle.
He would have changed the circle if he could,
The circle that was the grass track where he ran.
Twenty times a day he ran round the field
And still there was no winning post where the runner is cheered
    home.
Desperately he broke the tune,
But however he tried always the same melody crept up from the
    background,
The dragging step of a ploughman going home through the guttery
Headlands under an April-watery moon.
Religion, the fields and the fear of the Lord
And Ignorance giving him the coward's blow;
He dare not rise to pluck the fantasies
From the fruited Tree of Life. He bowed his head
And saw a wet weed twined about his toe.

V

Evening at the cross-roads –
Heavy heads nodding out words as wise
As the rumination of cows after milking.
From the ragged road surface a boy picks up
A piece of gravel and stares at it – and then
He flings it across the elm tree on to the railway.
It means nothing,
Not a damn thing.
Somebody is coming over the metal railway bridge
And his hobnailed boots on the arches sound like a gong
Calling men awake. But the bridge is too narrow –
The men lift their heads a moment. That was only John,
So they dream on.

Night in the elms, night in the grass.
O we are too tired to go home yet. Two cyclists pass
Talking loudly of Kitty and Molly –
Horses or women? wisdom or folly?

A door closes on an evicted dog
Where prayers begin in Barney Meegan's kitchen;
Rosie curses the cat between her devotions;
The daughter prays that she may have three wishes –
Health and wealth and love –
From the fairy who is faith or hope or compounds of.

At the cross-roads the crowd had thinned out:
Last words are uttered. There is no tomorrow;
No future but only time stretched for the mowing of the hay
Or putting an axle in the turf-barrow.

Patrick Maguire went home and made cocoa
And broke a chunk off the loaf of wheaten bread;
His mother called down to him to look again
And make sure that the hen-house was locked. His sister grunted
    in bed,
The sound of a sow taking up a new position.
Pat opened his trousers wide over the ashes
And dreamt himself to lewd sleepiness.
The clock ticked on. Time passes.

VI

Health and wealth and love he too dreamed of in May
As he sat on the railway slope and watched the children of the
    place
Picking up a primrose here and a daisy there –
They were picking up life's truth singly. But he dreamt of the
    Absolute envased bouquet –
All or nothing. And it was nothing. For God is not all
In one place, complete and labelled like a case in a railway store
Till Hope comes in and takes it on his shoulder –
O Christ, that is what you have done for us:
In a crumb of bread the whole mystery is.

He read the symbol too sharply and turned
From the five simple doors of sense
To the door whose combination lock has puzzled
Philosopher and priest and common dunce.

Men build their heavens as they build their circles
Of friends. God is in the bits and pieces of Everyday –
A kiss here and a laugh again, and sometimes tears,
A pearl necklace round the neck of poverty.

He sat on the railway slope and watched the evening,
Too beautifully perfect to use,
And his three wishes were three stones too sharp to sit on,
Too hard to carve. Three frozen idols of a speechless muse.

VII

'Now go to Mass and pray and confess your sins
And you'll have all the luck,' his mother said.
He listened to the lie that is a woman's screen
Around a conscience when soft thighs are spread.
And all the while she was setting up the lie
She trusted in Nature that never deceives.
But her son took it as the literal truth.
Religion's walls expand to the push of nature. Morality yields
To sense – but not in little tillage fields.

Life went on like that. One summer morning
Again through a hay-field on her way to the shop –
The grass was wet and over-leaned the path –
And Agnes held her skirts sensationally up,
And not because the grass was wet either.
A man was watching her, Patrick Maguire.
She was in love with passion and its weakness
And the wet grass could never cool the fire
That radiated from her unwanted womb
In that country, in that metaphysical land,
Where flesh was a thought more spiritual than music,
Among the stars – out of the reach of the peasant's hand.

Ah, but the priest was one of the people too –
A farmer's son – and surely he knew
The needs of a brother and sister.
Religion could not be a counter-irritant like a blister,

But the certain standard measured and known
By which a man might re-make his soul though all walls were
      down
And all earth's pedestalled gods thrown.

VIII

Sitting on a wooden gate,
Sitting on a wooden gate,
Sitting on a wooden gate,
He didn't care a damn.
Said whatever came into his head,
Said whatever came into his head,
Said whatever came into his head
And inconsequently sang.
Inconsequently sang,
While his world withered away.
He had a cigarette to smoke and a pound to spend
On drink the next Saturday.
His cattle were fat
And his horses all that
Midsummer grass could make them.
The young women ran wild
And dreamed of a child.
Joy dreams though the fathers might forsake them
But no one would take them,
No one would take them;
No man could ever see
That their skirts had loosed buttons,
Deliberately loosed buttons.
O the men were as blind as could be.
And Patrick Maguire
From his purgatory fire
Called the gods of the Christian to prove

That this twisted skein
Was the necessary pain
And not the rope that was strangling true love.

But sitting on a wooden gate
Sometime in July
When he was thirty-four or -five,
He gloried in the lie:
He made it read the way it should,
He made life read the evil good
While he cursed the ascetic brotherhood
Without knowing why.
Sitting on a wooden gate
All, all alone,
He sang and laughed
Like a man quite daft,
Or like a man on a channel raft
He fantasied forth his groan.
Sitting on a wooden gate,
Sitting on a wooden gate,
Sitting on a wooden gate
He rode in day-dream cars.
He locked his body with his knees
When the gate swung too much in the breeze,
But while he caught high ecstasies
Life slipped between the bars.

IX

He gave himself another year,
Something was bound to happen before then –
The circle would break down
And he would curve the new one to his own will.
A new rhythm is a new life

And in it marriage is hung and money.
He would be a new man walking through unbroken meadows
Of dawn in the year of One.

The poor peasant talking to himself in a stable door –
An ignorant peasant deep in dung.
What can the passers-by think otherwise?
Where is his silver bowl of knowledge hung?
Why should men be asked to believe in a soul
That is only the mark of a hoof in guttery gaps?
A man is what is written on the label.
And the passing world stares but no one stops
To look closer. So back to the growing crops
And the ridges he never loved.
Nobody will ever know how much tortured poetry the pulled
     weeds on the ridge wrote
Before they withered in the July sun,
Nobody will ever read the wild, sprawling, scrawling mad
     woman's signature,
The hysteria and the boredom of the enclosed nun of his thought.
Like the afterbirth of a cow stretched on a branch in the wind,
Life dried in the veins of these women and men:
The grey and grief and unlove,
The bones in the backs of their hands,
And the chapel pressing its low ceiling over them.

Sometimes they did laugh and see the sunlight,
A narrow slice of divine instruction.
Going along the river at the bend of Sunday
The trout played in the pools encouragement
To jump in love though death bait the hook.
And there would be girls sitting on the grass banks of lanes
Stretch-legged and lingering staring –
A man might take one of them if he had the courage.

But 'No' was in every sentence of their story
Except when the public-house came in and shouted its piece.

The yellow buttercups and the bluebells among the whin bushes
On rocks in the middle of ploughing
Was a bright spoke in the wheel
Of the peasant's mill.
The goldfinches on the railway paling were worth looking at –
A man might imagine then
Himself in Brazil and these birds the Birds of Paradise
And the Amazon and the romance traced on the school map lived
    again.

Talk in evening corners and under trees
Was like an old book found in a king's tomb.
The children gathered round like students and listened
And some of the saga defied the draught in the open tomb
And was not blown.

X

Their intellectual life consisted in reading
Reynolds' News or the *Sunday Dispatch*,
With sometimes an old almanac brought down from the ceiling
Or a school reader brown with the droppings of thatch.
The sporting results or the headlines of war
Was a humbug profound as the highbrow's Arcana.
Pat tried to be wise to the abstraction of all that
But its secret dribbled down his waistcoat like a drink from a strainer.
He wagered a bob each way on the Derby,
He got a straight tip from a man in a shop –
A double from the Guineas it was and thought himself
A master mathematician when one of them came up
And he could explain how much he'd have drawn

On the double if the second leg had followed the first.
He was betting on form and breeding, he claimed,
And the man that did that could never be burst.
After that they went on to the war, and the generals
On both sides were shown to be stupid as hell.
If he'd taken *that* road, they remarked of a Marshal,
He'd have . . . O they knew their geography well.
This was their university. Maguire was an undergraduate
Who dreamed from his lowly position of rising
To a professorship like Larry McKenna or Duffy
Or the pig-gelder Nallon whose knowledge was amazing.
'A treble, full multiple odds . . . That's flat porter . . .
My turnips are destroyed with the blackguardly crows . . .
Another one . . . No, you're wrong about that thing I was telling
    you . . .
Did you part with your filly, Jack? I heard that you sold her . . .'
The students were all savants by the time of pub-close.

XI

A year passed and another hurried after it
And Patrick Maguire was still six months behind life –
His mother six months ahead of it;
His sister straddle-legged across it: –
One leg in hell and the other in heaven
And between the purgatory of middle-aged virginity –
She prayed for release to heaven or hell.
His mother's voice grew thinner like a rust-worn knife
But it cut more venomously as it thinned,
It cut him up the middle till he became more woman than man,
And it cut through to his mind before the end.

Another field whitened in the April air
And the harrows rattled over the seed.

He gathered the loose stones off the ridges carefully
And grumbled to his men to hurry. He looked like a man who
    could give advice
To foolish young fellows. He was forty-seven,
And there was depth in his jaw and his voice was the voice of a
    great cattle-dealer,
A man with whom the fair-green gods break even.
'I think I ploughed that lea the proper depth,
She ought to give a crop if any land gives . . .
Drive slower with the foal-mare, Joe.'
Joe, a young man of imagined wives,
Smiled to himself and answered like a slave:
'You needn't fear or fret.
I'm taking her as easy, as easy as . . .
Easy there, Fanny, easy, pet.'

They loaded the day-scoured implements on the cart
As the shadows of poplars crookened the furrows.
It was the evening, evening. Patrick was forgetting to be lonely
As he used to be in Aprils long ago.
It was the menopause, the misery-pause.

The schoolgirls passed his house laughing every morning
And sometimes they spoke to him familiarly –
He had an idea. Schoolgirls of thirteen
Would see no political intrigue in an old man's friendship.
Love,
The heifer waiting to be nosed by the old bull.
That notion passed too – there was the danger of talk
And jails are narrower than the five-sod ridge
And colder than the black hills facing Armagh in February.
He sinned over the warm ashes again and his crime
The law's long arm could not serve with 'time'.

His face set like an old judge's pose:
Respectability and righteousness,
Stand for no nonsense.
The priest from the altar called Patrick Maguire's name
To hold the collecting box in the chapel door
During all the Sundays of May.
His neighbours envied him his holy rise,
But he walked down from the church with affected indifference
And took the measure of heaven angle-wise.

He still could laugh and sing,
But not the wild laugh or the abandoned harmony now
That called the world to new silliness from the top of a wooden gate
When thirty-five could take the sparrow's bow.
Let us be kind, let us be kind and sympathetic:
Maybe life is not for joking or for finding happiness in –
This tiny light in Oriental Darkness
Looking out chance windows of poetry or prayer.

And the grief and defeat of men like these peasants
Is God's way – maybe – and we must not want too much
To see.
The twisted thread is stronger than the wind-swept fleece.
And in the end who shall rest in truth's high peace?
Or whose is the world now, even now?
O let us kneel where the blind ploughman kneels
And learn to live without despairing
In a mud-walled space –
Illiterate, unknown and unknowing.
Let us kneel where he kneels
And feel what he feels.

One day he saw a daisy and he thought it
Reminded him of his childhood –

He stopped his cart to look at it.
Was there a fairy hiding behind it?

He helped a poor woman whose cow
Had died on her;
He dragged home a drunken man on a winter's night;
And one rare moment he heard the young people playing on the
    railway stile
And he wished them happiness and whatever they most desired
    from life.

He saw the sunlight and begrudged no man
His share of what the miserly soil and soul
Gives in a season to a ploughman.
And he cried for his own loss one late night on the pillow
And yet thanked the God who had arranged these things.

Was he then a saint?
A Matt Talbot of Monaghan?

His sister Mary Anne spat poison at the children
Who sometimes came to the door selling raffle tickets
For holy funds.
'Get out you little tramps!' she would scream
As she shook to the hens an apronful of crumbs,
But Patrick often put his hand deep down
In his trouser-pocket and fingered out a penny
Or maybe a tobacco-stained caramel.
'You're soft,' said the sister, 'with other people's money;
It's not a bit funny.'

The cards are shuffled and the deck
Laid flat for cutting – 'Tom Malone,
Cut for trump. I think we'll make
This game, the last, a tanner one.

Hearts. Right. I see you're breaking
Your two-year-old. Play quick, Maguire,
The clock there says it's half-past ten –
Kate, throw another sod on that fire.'
One of the card-players laughs and spits
Into the flame across a shoulder.
Outside, a noise like a rat
Among the hen-roosts. The cock crows over
The frosted townland of the night.
Eleven o'clock and still the game
Goes on and the players seem to be
Drunk in an Orient opium den.
Midnight, one o'clock, two.
Somebody's leg has fallen asleep.
'What about home? Maguire, are you
Using your double-tree this week?
Why? do you want it? Play the ace.
There's it, and that's the last card for me.
A wonderful night, we had. Duffy's place
Is very convenient. Is that a ghost or a tree?'
And so they go home with dragging feet
And their voices rumble like laden carts.
And they are happy as the dead or sleeping . . .
I should have led that ace of hearts.

XII

The fields were bleached white,
The wooden tubs full of water
Were white in the winds
That blew through Brannagan's Gap on their way from Siberia;
The cows on the grassless heights
Followed the hay that had wings –
The February fodder that hung itself on the black branches

Of the hilltop hedge.
A man stood beside a potato-pit
And clapped his arms
And pranced on the crisp roots
And shouted to warm himself.
Then he buck-leaped about the potatoes
And scooped them into a basket.
He looked like a bucking suck-calf
Whose spine was being tickled.
Sometimes he stared across the bogs
And sometimes he straightened his back and vaguely whistled
A tune that weakened his spirit
And saddened his terrier dog's.
A neighbour passed with a spade on his shoulder
And Patrick Maguire, bent like a bridge,
Whistled good morning under his oxter,
And the man the other side of the hedge
Champed his spade on the road at his toes
And talked an old sentimentality
While the wind blew under his clothes.

The mother sickened and stayed in bed all day,
Her head hardly dented the pillow, so light and thin it had worn,
But she still enquired after the household affairs.
She held the strings of her children's Punch and Judy, and when a
    mouth opened
It was her truth that the dolls would have spoken
If they hadn't been made of wood and tin –
'Did you open the barn door, Pat, to let the young calves in?'
The priest called to see her every Saturday
And she told him her troubles and fears:
'If Mary Anne was settled I'd die in peace –
I'm getting on in years.'
'You were a good woman,' said the priest,

'And your children will miss you when you're gone.
The likes of you this parish never knew,
I'm sure they'll not forget the work you've done.'
She reached five bony crooks under the tick –
'Five pounds for Masses – won't you say them quick.'
She died one morning in the beginning of May
And a shower of sparrow-notes was the litany for her dying.
The holy water was sprinkled on the bed-clothes
And her children stood around the bed and cried because it was
    too late for crying.
A mother dead! The tired sentiment:
'Mother, Mother' was a shallow pool
Where sorrow hardly could wash its feet . . .
Mary Anne came away from the deathbed and boiled the calves
    their gruel.
O what was I doing when the procession passed?
Where was I looking?
Young women and men
And I might have joined them.
Who bent the coin of my destiny
That it stuck in the slot?
I remember a night we walked
Through the moon of Donaghmoyne,
Four of us seeking adventure –
It was midsummer forty years ago.
Now I know
The moment that gave the turn to my life.
O Christ! I am locked in a stable with pigs and cows for ever.

XIII

The world looks on
And talks of the peasant:
The peasant has no worries;
In his little lyrical fields
He ploughs and sows;
He eats fresh food,
He loves fresh women,
He is his own master;
As it was in the Beginning,
The simpleness of peasant life.
The birds that sing for him are eternal choirs,
Everywhere he walks there are flowers.
His heart is pure,
His mind is clear,
He can talk to God as Moses and Isaiah talked –
The peasant who is only one remove from the beasts he drives.
The travellers stop their cars to gape over the green bank into his
     fields: –

There is the source from which all cultures rise,
And all religions,
There is the pool in which the poet dips
And the musician.
Without the peasant base civilization must die,
Unless the clay is in the mouth the singer's singing is useless.
The travellers touch the roots of the grass and feel renewed
When they grasp the steering wheels again.
The peasant is the unspoiled child of Prophecy,
The peasant is all virtues – let us salute him without irony –
The peasant ploughman who is half a vegetable,
Who can react to sun and rain and sometimes even

Regret that the Maker of Light had not touched him more
    intensely,
Brought him up from the sub-soil to an existence
Of conscious joy. He was not born blind.
He is not always blind: sometimes the cataract yields
To sudden stone-falling or the desire to breed.

The girls pass along the roads
And he can remember what man is,
But there is nothing he can do.
Is there nothing he can do?
Is there no escape?
No escape, no escape.

The cows and horses breed,
And the potato-seed
Gives a bud and a root and rots
In the good mother's way with her sons;
The fledged bird is thrown
From the nest – on its own.
But the peasant in his little acres is tied
To a mother's womb by the wind-toughened navel-cord
Like a goat tethered to the stump of a tree –
He circles around and around wondering why it should be.
No crash,
No drama.
That was how his life happened.
No mad hooves galloping in the sky,
But the weak, washy way of true tragedy –
A sick horse nosing around the meadow for a clean place to die.

XIV

We may come out into the October reality, Imagination,
The sleety wind no longer slants to the black hill where Maguire
And his men are now collecting the scattered harness and baskets.
The dog sitting on a wisp of dry stalks
Watches them through the shadows.
'Back in, back in.' One talks to the horse as to a brother.
Maguire himself is patting a potato-pit against the weather –
An old man fondling a new-piled grave:
'Joe, I hope you didn't forget to hide the spade
For there's rogues in the townland. Hide it flat in a furrow.
I think we ought to be finished by tomorrow.'
Their voices through the darkness sound like voices from a cave,
A dull thudding far away, futile, feeble, far away,
First cousins to the ghosts of the townland.

A light stands in a window. Mary Anne
Has the table set and the tea-pot waiting in the ashes.
She goes to the door and listens and then she calls
From the top of the haggard-wall:
'What's keeping you
And the cows to be milked and all the other work there's to do?'
'All right, all right,
We'll not stay here all night.'

Applause, applause,
The curtain falls.
Applause, applause
From the homing carts and the trees
And the bawling cows at the gates.
From the screeching water-hens
And the mill-race heavy with the Lammas floods curving over the
    weir.

A train at the station blowing off steam
And the hysterical laughter of the defeated everywhere.
Night, and the futile cards are shuffled again.
Maguire spreads his legs over the impotent cinders that wake no
    manhood now
And he hardly looks to see which card is trump.
His sister tightens her legs and her lips and frizzles up
Like the wick of an oil-less lamp.
The curtain falls –
Applause, applause.

Maguire is not afraid of death, the Church will light him a candle
To see his way through the vaults and he'll understand the
Quality of the clay that dribbles over his coffin.
He'll know the names of the roots that climb down to tickle his
    feet.
And he will feel no different than when he walked through
    Donaghmoyne.
If he stretches out a hand – a wet clod,
If he opens his nostrils – a dungy smell;
If he opens his eyes once in a million years –
Through a crack in the crust of the earth he may see a face
    nodding in
Or a woman's legs. Shut them again for that sight is sin.

He will hardly remember that life happened to him –
Something was brighter a moment. Somebody sang in the
    distance.
A procession passed down a mesmerized street.
He remembers names like Easter and Christmas
By the colour his fields were.
Maybe he will be born again, a bird of an angel's conceit
To sing the gospel of life
To a music as flightily tangent

As a tune on an oboe.
And the serious look of the fields will have changed to the leer of a
     hobo
Swaggering celestially home to his three wishes granted.
Will that be? will that be?
Or is the earth right that laughs, haw haw,
And does not believe
In an unearthly law.
The earth that says:
Patrick Maguire, the old peasant, can neither be damned nor
     glorified;
The graveyard in which he will lie will be just a deep-drilled
     potato-field
Where the seed gets no chance to come through
To the fun of the sun.
The tongue in his mouth is the root of a yew.
Silence, silence. The story is done.

He stands in the doorway of his house
A ragged sculpture of the wind,
October creaks the rotted mattress,
The bedposts fall. No hope. No lust.
The hungry fiend
Screams the apocalypse of clay
In every corner of this land.

Lough Derg

From Cavan and from Leitrim and from Mayo,
From all the thin-faced parishes where hills
Are perished noses running peaty water,
They come to Lough Derg to fast and pray and beg
With all the bitterness of nonentities, and the envy
Of the inarticulate when dealing with an artist.
Their hands push closed the doors that God holds open.
Love-sunlit is an enchanter in June's hours
And flowers and light. These to shopkeepers and small lawyers
Are heresies up beauty's sleeve.

The naïve and simple go on pilgrimage too,
Lovers trying to take God's truth for granted . . .
Listen to the chanted
Evening devotions in the limestone church,
For this is Lough Derg, St Patrick's Purgatory.
He came to this island-acre of greenstone once
To be shut of the smug too-faithful. The story
Is different now:
Solicitors praying for cushy jobs,
To be County Registrar or Coroner;
Shopkeepers threatened with sharper rivals
Than any hook-nosed foreigner;
Mothers whose daughters are Final Medicals,
Too heavy-hipped for thinking;
Wives whose husbands have angina pectoris,
Wives whose husbands have taken to drinking.

But there were the sincere as well,
The innocent who feared the hell

Of sin. The girl who had won
A lover and the girl who had none
Were both in trouble,
Trying to encave in the rubble
Of these rocks the Real,
The part that can feel.
And the half-pilgrims too,
They who are the true
Spirit of Ireland, who joke
Through the Death-mask and take
Virgins of heaven or flesh,
Were on Lough Derg Island
Wanting some half-wish.

Over the black waves of the lake trip the last echoes
Of the bell that has shooed through the chapel door
The last pilgrims, like hens to roost.
The sun through Fermanagh's furze fingers
Looks now on the deserted penance rings of stone
Where only John Flood on St Kevin's Bed lingers
With the sexton's heaven-sure stance, the man who knows
The ins and outs of religion . . .
'Hail glorious St Patrick' a girl sings above
The old-man drone of the harmonium.
The rosary is said and Benediction.
The Sacramental sun turns round and 'Holy, Holy, Holy'
The pilgrims cry, striking their breasts in Purgatory.

The same routine and ritual now
As serves for street processions or Congresses
That take all shapes of souls as a living theme
In a novel refuses nothing. No truth oppresses.

Women and men in bare feet turn again
To the iron crosses and the rutted Beds,
Their feet are swollen and their bellies empty –
But something that is Ireland's secret leads
These petty mean people,
For here's the day of a poor soul freed
To a marvellous beauty above its head.
The Castleblayney grocer trapped in the moment's need
Puts out a hand and writes what he cannot read,
A wisdom astonished at every turn
By some angel that writes in the oddest words.
When he will walk again in Muckno Street
He'll hear from the kitchens of fair-day eating houses
In the after-bargain carouses
News from a country beyond the range of birds.

The lake waves caught the concrete stilts of the Basilica
That spread like a bulldog's hind paws. A Leitrim man,
With a face as sad as a flooded hay-field,
Leaned in an angle of the walls with his rosary beads in his hands.

Beside St Brigid's Cross – an ancient relic,
A fragment of the Middle Ages set
Into the modern masonry of the conventional Basilica
Where everything is ordered and correct –
A queue of pilgrims waiting to renounce
The World, the Flesh, the Devil and all his house.

Like young police recruits being measured
Each pilgrim flattened backwards to the wall
And stretched his arms wide
As he cried:
'I renounce the World, the Flesh and the Devil';
Three times they cried out. A country curate

Stared with a curate leer – he was proud.
The booted
Prior passes by ignoring all the crowd.

'I renounce the World,' a young woman cried.
Her breasts stood high in the pagan sun.
'I renounce . . .' an old monk followed. Then a fat lawyer.
They rejected one by one
The music of Time's choir.

A half-pilgrim looked up at the Carrara marbles,
St Patrick wearing an alb with no stitch dropped.
Once he held a shamrock in his hand
But the stem was flawed and it got lost.

St Brigid and the Blessed Virgin flanked
Ireland's national apostle
On the south-west of the island on the gravel-path
Opposite the men's hostel.

Around the island like soldiers quartered round a barrack-
    yard
There were houses, and a stall where agnisties
And Catholic Truth pamphlets were sold,
And at the pier end, the grey chapel of St Mary's.

The middle of the island looked like the memory
Of some village evicted by the Famine,
Some corner of a field beside a well,
Old stumps of walls where a stunted boortree is growing.
These were the holy cells of saintly men –
O that was the place where Mickey Fehan lived
And the Reillys before they went to America in the Fifties.
No, this is Lough Derg in County Donegal –
So much alike is our historical

And spiritual pattern, a heap
Of stones anywhere is consecrated
By love's terrible need.

On Lough Derg, too, the silver strands
Of the individual sometimes show
Through the fabric of prison anonymity;
One man's private trouble transcending the divinity
Of the prayer-locked multitude,
A vein of humanity that can bleed
Through the thickest hide.
And such a plot unfolds a moment, so –

In a crevice between the houses and the lake
A tall red-headed man of thirty slouches,
A half-pilgrim who hated prayer,
All truth for which St Patrick's Purgatory vouches.
He was a small farmer who was fond of literature
In a country-schoolmaster way.
He skimmed the sentiment of every pool of experience
And talked heresy lightly from distances
Where nothing was terrifyingly Today,
Where he felt he could be safe and say or sin –
But Christ sometimes bleeds in the museum.
It was the first day of his pilgrimage.
He came to Lough Derg to please the superstition
Which says, 'At least the thing can do no harm',
Yet he alone went out with Jesus fishing.

An ex-monk from Dublin, a broad-faced man
With his Franciscan habit sweeping was a pilgrim,
A sad priest staggering in a megrim
Between doubt and vanity's courtesan.
He had fallen once and secretly, no shame
Tainted the young girl's name,

A convent schoolgirl knowing
Nothing of earth sowing.
He took her three times
As in his day-dreams
These things happened.
Three times finds all
The notes of body's madrigal.
'Twas a failing otherwise
Lost him his priestly faculties.

Barefoot in the kitchen
Of John Flood's cottage
Where the girls of Donegal sat, laughing round on stools,
And iron cranes and crooks
Were loaded with black pots,
And holy-looking women kept going in and out of the rooms
As though some man was a-waking . . .
The red-haired man came in
And saw among the loud, cold women one who
Was not a Holy Biddy
With a rat-trap on her diddy,
But something from the unconverted kingdom,
The beauty that has turned
Convention into forests
Where Adam wanders deranged with half a memory;
And red-haired Robert Fitzsimons
Saw Aggie Meegan, and quietly
An angel was turning over the pages of Mankind's history.
He must have her, she was waiting
By the unprotected gable
Of asceticism's granite castle. The masonry's down
And the sun coming in is blood,
The green of trees is lust,
He saw from the unpeopled country into a town.

Let beauty bag or burst,
The sharp points of truth may not be versed
Too smoothly, but the truth must go in as it occurred,
A bulb of light in the shadows of Lough Derg.

The first evening they prayed till nine o'clock
Around the gravel rings, a hundred decades
Of rosaries, until they hardly knew what words meant –
Their own names when they spoke them sounded mysterious.
They knelt and prayed and rose and prayed
And circled the crosses and kissed the stones
Never looking away from the brimstone bitterness
To the little islands of Pan held in the crooked elbow of the lake.
They closed their eyes to Donegal and the white houses
On the slope of the northern hills.

And these pilgrims of a Western reason
Were not pursuing French-hot miracles.
There were hundreds of them tripping one another
Upon the pilgrim way (O God of Truth,
Keep him who tells this story straight,
Let no cheap insincerity shape his mouth).
These men and boys were not led there
By priests of Maynooth or stories of Italy or Spain,
For this is the penance of the poor
Who know what beauty hides in misery
As beggars, fools and eastern fakirs know.

Black tea, dry bread.
Yesterday's pilgrims went upstairs to bed
And as they slept
The vigil in St Patrick's prison was kept
By the others. The Evening Star
Looked into Purgatory whimsically. Night dreams are

Simple and catching as music-hall tunes
Of the Nineties. We'll ramble through the brambles of
　　starry-strange Junes.

On a seat beside the women's hostel four men
Sat and talked spare minutes away;
It was like Sunday evening on a country road
Light and gay.
The talk was 'There's a man
Who must be twenty stone weight – a horrid size . . .'
'Larry O'Duff . . . yes, like a balloon
Or a new tick of chaff . . . Lord, did anyone ever see clearer skies?'
'No rain a while yet, Joe,
And the turnips could be doing with a sup, you know.'
And in the women's talk, too, was woven
Such earth to cool the burning brain of Heaven.
On the steps of the church the monks talked
To Robert of art, music, literature.
'Genius is not measured,' he said,
'In prudent feet and inches,
Old Justice burns the work of Raphael –
Justice was God until he saw His Son
Falling in love with earth's fantastic one,
The woman in whose dunghill of emotion
Grow flowers of poetry, music and the old
Kink in the mind; the fascination
Of sin troubled the mind of God
Until He thought of Charity . . .
Have you known Charity? Have I?'
Aggie Meegan passed by
To vigil. Robert was puzzled. Where
Grew the germ of this crooked prayer?
The girl was thrilling as joy's despair.

A schoolmaster from Roscommon led
The vigil prayers that night.
'Hail Queen of Heaven' they sang at twelve.
Someone snored near the porch. A bright
Moon sailed in from the County Tyrone
By the water route that he might make
Queer faces in the stained-glassed windows. Why should sun
Have all the fun?
'Our vows of Baptism we again take . . .'
Every Rosary brought the morning nearer.
The schoolmaster looked at his watch and said:
'Out now for a mouthful of fresh air –
A ten-minute break to clear the head.'

It was cold in the rocky draughts between the houses.
Old women tried
To pull bare feet close to their bellies.
Three o'clock rang from the Prior's house clock.
In the hostels pilgrims slept away a three-day fast.

On the cell-wall beside the sycamore tree,
The tree that never knew a bird,
Aggie sat fiddling with her Rosary
And doubting the power of Lough Derg
To save the season's rose of life
With the ponderous fingers of prayer's philosophy.

Robert was a philosopher, a false one
Who ever takes a sledge to swat a fly.
He talked to the girls as a pedant professor
Talking in a university.
The delicate precise immediacy
That sees a flower half a foot away
He could not learn. He spoke to Aggie
Of powers, passions, with the *naïveté*

Of a ploughman. She did not understand –
She only knew that she could hold his hand
If he stood closer. 'Virtue is sublime,'
He said, 'and it is virtue is the frame
Of all love and learning . . .'
'I want to tell you something,' she whispered,
'Because you are different and will know . . .'
'You don't need to tell me anything, you could not,
For your innocence is pure glass that I see through.'
'You'd be surprised,' she smiled. O God, he gasped
To his soul, what could she mean by that?
They watched the lake waves clapping cold hands together
And saw the morning breaking as it breaks
Over a field where a man is watching a calving cow.
New life, new day.
A half-pilgrim saw it as a rabbiter
Poaching in wood sees
Primeval magic among the trees.

The rusty cross of St Patrick had a dozen
Devotees clustered around it at four o'clock.
Bare knees were going round St Brendan's Bed.
A boy was standing like a ballet dancer poised on the rock
Under the belfry; he stared over at Donegal
Where the white houses on the side of the hills
Popped up like mushrooms in September.
The sun was smiling on a thousand hayfields
That hour, and he must have thought Lough Derg
More unreasonable than ordinary stone.
Perhaps it was an iceberg
That he had glanced at on his journey from Japan,
But the iceberg filled a glass of water
And poured it to the honour of the sun.
Lough Derg in the dawn poured rarer cups. Prayer

And fast that makes the sourest drink rare.
Was that St Paul
Riding his ass down a lane in Donegal?
Christ was lately dead,
Men were afraid
With a new fear, the fear
Of love. There was a laugh freed
For ever and for ever. The Apostles' Creed
Was a fireside poem, the talk of the town . . .
They remember a man who has seen Christ in his thorny crown.

John Flood came out and climbed the rock to ring
His bell for six o'clock. He spoke to the pilgrims:
'Was the night fine?'
'Wonderful, wonderful,' they answered, 'not too cold –
Thank God we have the worst part over us.'

The bell brought the sleepers from their cubicles.
Grey-faced boatmen were getting out a boat.
Mass was said. Another day began.
The penance wheel turned round again.
Pilgrims went out in boats, singing
'O Fare Thee Well, Lough Derg' as they waved
Affection to the persecuting stones.

The Prior went with them – suavely, goodily,
Priestly, painfully directing the boats.
They who were left behind
Felt like the wellwishers who keep house when the funeral
Has left for the chapel.

Lough Derg overwhelmed the individual imagination
And the personal tragedy.
Only God thinks of the dying sparrow
In the middle of a war.

The ex-monk, farmer and the girl
Melted in the crowd
Where only God, the poet,
Followed with interest till he found
Their secret, and constructed from
The chaos of its fire
A reasonable document.

A man's the centre of the world,
A man is not an anonymous
Member of the general public.
The Communion of Saints
Is a Communion of individuals.
God the Father is the Father
Of each one of us.

Then there was war, the slang, the contemporary touch,
The ideologies of the daily papers.
They must seem realer, Churchill, Stalin, Hitler,
Than ideas in the contemplative cloister.
The battles where ten thousand men die
Are more significant than a peasant's emotional problem.
But wars will be merely dry bones in histories
And these common people real living creatures in it
On the unwritten spaces between the lines.
A man throws himself prostrate
And God lies down beside him like a woman
Consoling the hysteria of her lover
That sighs his passion emptily:
'The next time, love, you shall faint in me.'

'Don't ask for life,' the monk said.
'If you meet her
Be easy with your affection;
She's a traitor

To those who love too much
As I have done.'
'What have you done?' said Robert,
'That you've come
To St Patrick's Purgatory?'
The monk told his story
Of how he thought that he
Could make reality
Of the romance of the books
That told of Popes,
Men of genius who drew
Wild colours on the flat page. He knew
Now that madness is not knowing
That laws for the mown hay
Will not serve that which is growing.
Through Lough Derg's fast and meditation
He learned the wisdom of his generation.
He was satisfied now his heart
Was free from the coquetry of art.

Something was unknown
To Robert, not long,
For Aggie told him all
That hour as they sat on the wall
Of Brendan's cell:
Birth, bastardy and murder –
He only heard rocks crashing distantly
When John Flood rang the midday bell.

Now the three of them got out of the story altogether
Almost. Now they were not three egotists
But part of the flood of humanity,
Anonymous, never to write or be written.
They vanish among the forests and we see them

Appearing among the trees for seconds.
Lough Derg rolls its caravan before us
And as the pilgrims pass their thoughts are reckoned.
St Patrick was there, that peasant-faced man,
Whose image was embroidered on political banners
In the days of the AOH and John Redmond.
A kindly soft man this Patrick was, like a farmer
To whom no man might be afraid to tell a story
Of bawdy life as it goes in country places.
Was St Patrick like that?
A shamrock in a politician's hat
Yesterday. Today
The sentimentality of an Urban Councillor
Moving an address of welcome to the Cardinal.
All Ireland's Patricks were present on Lough Derg,
All Ireland that froze for want of Europe.

'And who are you?' said the poet speaking to
The old Leitrim man.
He said, 'I can tell you
What I am.
Servant girls bred my servility:
When I stoop
It is my mother's mother's mother's mother
Each one in turn being called in to spread –
"Wider with your legs," the master of the house said.
Domestic servants taken back and front.
That's why I'm servile. It is not the poverty
Of soil in Leitrim that makes me raise my hat
To fools with fifty pounds in a paper bank.
Domestic servants, no one has told
Their generations as it is, as I
Show the cowardice of the man whose mothers were whored
By five generations of capitalist and lord.'

Time passed.
Three boatloads of Dublin's unemployed came in
At three o'clock led by a priest from Thomas Street
To glutton over the peat-filtered water
And sit back drunk when jobs are found
In the Eternal factory where the boss
Himself must punch the clock.

And the day crawled lazily
Along the orbit of Purgatory.

A baker from Rathfriland,
A solicitor from Derry,
A parish priest from Wicklow,
A civil servant from Kerry,
Sat on the patch of grass,
Their stations for the day
Completed – all things arranged,
Nothing in doubt, nothing gone astray.

O the boredom of Purgatory,
Said the poet then,
This piety that hangs like a fool's, unthought,
This certainty in men,
This three days too-goodness,
Too-neighbourly cries,
Temptation to murder
Mediocrities.

The confession boxes in St Mary's chapel hum
And it is evening now. Prose prayers become
Odes and sonnets.
There is a shrine with money heaped upon it
Before Our Lady of Miraculous Succour.

A woman said her litany:
That my husband may get his health
   We beseech thee hear us
That my son Joseph may pass the Intermediate
   We beseech thee hear us
That my daughter Eileen may do well at her music
   We beseech thee hear us
That her aunt may remember us in her will
   We beseech thee hear us
That there may be good weather for the hay
   We beseech thee hear us
That my indigestion may be cured
   We beseech thee hear us
O Mother of Perpetual Succour! in temptation
   Be you near us.
And some deep prayers were shaped like sonnets –

O good St Anthony, your poor client asks
That he may have one moment in his arms
The girl I am thinking of this minute –
I'd love her even if she had no farms
Or a four-footed beast in a stable;
Her father is old, doting down the lanes,
There isn't anyone as able
As I am for cocking hay or cleaning drains.
All this that I am is an engine running
Light down the narrow-gauge railway of life.
St Anthony, I ask for Mary Gunning
Of Rathdrumskean to be my wife.
My strength is a skull battering the wall
Where a remand-prisoner is losing his soul.

St Anne, I am a young girl from Castleblayney,
One of a farmer's six grown daughters.

Our little farm, when the season's rainy,
Is putty spread on stones. The surface waters
Soak all the fields of this north-looking townland.
Last year we lost our acre of potatoes;
And my mother with unmarried daughters round her
Is soaked like our soil in savage natures.
She tries to be as kind as any mother
But what can a mother be in such a house
With arguments going on and such a bother
About the half-boiled pots and unmilked cows.
O Patron of the pure woman who lacks a man,
Let me be free I beg of you, St Anne.

O Sacred Heart of Jesus, I ask of you
A job so I can settle down and marry;
I want to live a decent life. And through
The flames of St Patrick's Purgatory
I go offering every stone-bruise, all my hunger;
In the back-room of my penance I am weaving
An inside-shirt for charity. How longer
Must a fifty-shilling-a-week job be day-dreaming?
The dole and empty minds and empty pockets,
Cup Finals seen from the branches of a tree,
Old films that break the eye-balls in their sockets,
A toss-pit. This is life for such as me.
And I know a girl and I know a room to be let
And a job in a builder's yard to be given yet.

I have sinned old; my lust's a running sore
That drains away my strength. Each morning shout:
'Last night will be the last!' At fifty-four
A broken will's a bone that will not knit.
I slip on the loose rubble of remorse
And grasp at tufts of cocksfoot grass that yield,

My belly is a bankrupt's purse.
My mind is a thrice-failed cropping field
Where the missed ridges give out their ecstasy
To weeds that seed through gaps of indiscretion,
Nettles where barley or potatoes should be.
I set my will in Communion and Confession
But still the sore is dribbling blood, and will,
In spite of penance, prayer and canticle.

This was the banal
Beggary that God heard. Was he bored
As men are with the poor? Christ Lord
Hears in the voices of the meanly poor
Homeric utterances, poetry sweeping through.

More pilgrims came that evening
From the pier.
The old ones watched the boats come
And smothered the ridiculous cheer
That breaks, like a hole in pants,
Where the heroic armies advance.

Somebody brought a newspaper
With news of war.
When they lived in Time they knew
What men killed each other for –
Was it something different in the spelling
Of a useless law?

A man under the campanile said:
'Kipper is fish – nice.'
Somebody else talked of Dempsey:
'Greater than Tunney.' Then a girl's voice
Called: 'You'll get cigarettes inside.'

It was six o'clock in the evening.
Robert sat looking over the lake
Seeing the green islands that were his morning hope
And his evening despair.
The sharp knife of Jansen
Cuts all the green branches.
Not sunlight comes in
But the hot-iron sin,
Branding the shame
Of a beast in the Name
Of Christ on the breast
Of a child of the West.
It was this he had read.
All day he was smitten
By this foul legend written
In the fields, in the skies,
In the sanctuaries.
But now the green tree
Of humanity
Was leafing again,
Forgiveness of sin.
A shading hand over
The brow of the lover.

And as the hours of Lough Derg's time
Stretch long enough to hold a generation,
He sat beside her and promised that no word
Of what he knew should ever be heard.
The bell at nine o'clock closed the last station,
The pilgrims kissed goodbye to stone and clay.
The Prior had declared the end of day.

Morning from the hostel windows was like the morning
In some village street after a dance carouse,

Debauchees of Venus and Bacchus
Half-alive stumbling wearily out of a bleary house.
So these pilgrims stumbled below in the sun
Out of God's public-house.

The Mass was said.
Pilgrims smiled at one another:
How good God was,
How much a loving Father!
How wonderful the punishing stones were!
Another hour and the boats will sail
Into the port of Time.
Are you not glad you came?

John Flood stared at the sky
And shook his proud head knowingly.
No storm, nor rain.
The boats are ready to sail.

The monk appears once more,
Not trailing his robe as before,
But different, his pride gone,
Green hope growing where the feet of Pan
Had hoofed the grass.

Lough Derg, St Patrick's Purgatory in Donegal,
Christendom's purge. Heretical
Around the edges: the centre's hard
As the commonsense of a flamboyant bard.
The twentieth century blows across it now,
But deeply it has kept an ancient vow.
It knows the secret of pain –
O moralist, your preaching is in vain
To tell men of the germ in the grain.

All happened on Lough Derg as it is written
In June nineteen forty-two
When the Germans were fighting outside Rostov.
The poet wrote it down as best he knew,
As integral and completed as the emotion
Of men and women cloaking a burning emotion
In the rags of the commonplace will permit him.
He too was one of them. He too denied
The half of him that was his pride
Yet found it waiting, and the half untrue
Of this story is his pride's rhythm.

The turnips were a-sowing in the fields around Pettigo
As our train passed through.
A horse-cart stopped near the eye of the railway bridge.
By Monaghan and Cavan and Dundalk
By Bundoran and by Omagh the pilgrims went;
And three sad people had found the key to the lock
Of God's delight in disillusionment.

Advent

We have tested and tasted too much, lover –
Through a chink too wide there comes in no wonder.
But here in this Advent-darkened room
Where the dry black bread and the sugarless tea
Of penance will charm back the luxury
Of a child's soul, we'll return to Doom
The knowledge we stole but could not use.

And the newness that was in every stale thing
When we looked at it as children: the spirit-shocking
Wonder in a black slanting Ulster hill,
Or the prophetic astonishment in the tedious talking
Of an old fool, will awake for us and bring
You and me to the yard gate to watch the whins
And the bog-holes, cart-tracks, old stables where Time begins.

O after Christmas we'll have no need to go searching
For the difference that sets an old phrase burning –
We'll hear it in the whispered argument of a churning
Or in the streets where the village boys are lurching.
And we'll hear it among simple, decent men, too,
Who barrow dung in gardens under trees,
Wherever life pours ordinary plenty.
Won't we be rich, my love and I, and please
God we shall not ask for reason's payment,
The why of heart-breaking strangeness in dreeping hedges,
Nor analyse God's breath in common statement.
We have thrown into the dust-bin the clay-minted wages
Of pleasure, knowledge and the conscious hour –
And Christ comes with a January flower.

Beyond the Headlines

Then I saw the wild geese flying
In fair formation to their bases in Inchicore,
And I knew that these wings would outwear the wings of war,
And a man's simple thoughts outlive the day's loud lying.

Don't fear, don't fear, I said to my soul:
The Bedlam of Time is an empty bucket rattled,
'Tis you who will say in the end who best battled.
Only they who fly home to God have flown at all.

Consider the Grass Growing

Consider the grass growing
As it grew last year and the year before,
Cool about the ankles like summer rivers,
When we walked on a May evening through the meadows
To watch the mare that was going to foal.

Threshing Morning

On an apple-ripe September morning
Through the mist-chill fields I went
With a pitchfork on my shoulder
Less for use than for devilment.

The threshing mill was set-up, I knew,
In Cassidy's haggard last night,
And we owed them a day at the threshing
Since last year. O it was delight

To be paying bills of laughter
And chaffy gossip in kind
With work thrown in to ballast
The fantasy-soaring mind.

As I crossed the wooden bridge I wondered,
As I looked into the drain,
If ever a summer morning should find me
Shovelling up eels again.

And I thought of the wasps' nest in the bank
And how I got chased one day
Leaving the drag and the scraw-knife behind,
How I covered my face with hay.

The wet leaves of the cocksfoot
Polished my boots as I
Went round by the glistening bog-holes
Lost in unthinking joy.

I'll be carrying bags today, I mused,
The best job at the mill,
With plenty of time to talk of our loves
As we wait for the bags to fill . . .

Maybe Mary might call round . . .
And then I came to the haggard gate,
And I knew as I entered that I had come
Through fields that were part of no earthly estate.

Patrick Kavanagh

October 1943

And the rain coming down, and the rain coming down!
How lovely it falls on the rick well headed,
On potato pits thatched, on the turf clamps home,
On the roofs of the byre where the cows are bedded!

And the sun shining down, and the sun shining down!
How bright on the turnip leaves, on the stubble –
Where turkeys tip-toe across the ridges –
In this corner of peace in a world of trouble.

Peace

And sometimes I am sorry when the grass
Is growing over the stones in quiet hollows
And the cocksfoot leans across the rutted cart-pass,
That I am not the voice of country fellows
Who now are standing by some headland talking
Of turnips and potatoes or young corn
Or turf banks stripped for victory.
Here Peace is still hawking
His coloured combs and scarves and beads of horn.

Upon a headland by a whinny hedge
A hare sits looking down a leaf-lapped furrow;
There's an old plough upside-down on a weedy ridge

And someone is shouldering home a saddle-harrow.
Out of that childhood country what fools climb
To fight with tyrants Love and Life and Time?

A Wreath for Tom Moore's Statue

The cowardice of Ireland is in his statue,
No poet's honoured when they wreathe this stone,
An old shopkeeper who has dealt in the marrow-bone
Of his neighbours looks at you.
Dim-eyed, degenerate, he is admiring his god,
The bank-manager who pays his monthly confession,
The tedious narrative of a mediocrity's passion,
The shallow, safe sins that never become a flood
To sweep themselves away. From under
His coat-lapels the vermin creep as Joyce
Noted in passing on his exile's way.
In the wreathing of this stone now I wonder
If there is not somehow the worship of the lice
That crawl upon the seven-deadened clay.

They put a wreath upon the dead
For the dead will wear the cap of any racket,
The corpse will not put his elbows through his jacket
Or contradict the words some liar has said.
The corpse can be fitted out to deceive –
Fake thoughts, fake love, fake ideal,
And rogues can sell its guaranteed appeal,
Guaranteed to work and never come alive.

The poet would not stay poetical
And his humility was far from being pliable,
Voluptuary tomorrow, today ascetical,
His morning gentleness was the evening's rage.
But here we give you death, the old reliable
Whose white blood cannot blot the respectable page.

Some clay the lice have stirred
Falls now for ever into hell's lousy hollows.
The terrible peace is that follows
The annihilation of the flesh-rotted word.
But hope! the poet comes again to build
A new city high above lust and logic,
The trucks of language overflow and magic
At every turn of the living road is spilled.

The sense is over-sense. No need more
To analyse, to controvert or turn
The laugh against the cynic's leer of power.
In his own city now he lives before
The clay earth was made, an Adam never born,
His light unprisoned in a dinner-hour.

Pegasus

My soul was an old horse
Offered for sale in twenty fairs.
I offered him to the Church – the buyers
Were little men who feared his unusual airs.

One said: 'Let him remain unbid
In the wind and rain and hunger
Of sin and we will get him –
With the winkers thrown in – for nothing.'

Then the men of State looked at
What I'd brought for sale.
One minister, wondering if
Another horse-body would fit the tail
That he'd kept for sentiment –
The relic of his own soul –
Said, 'I will graze him in lieu of his labour.'
I lent him for a week or more
And he came back a hurdle of bones,
Starved, overworked, in despair.
I nursed him on the roadside grass
To shape him for another fair.

I lowered my price. I stood him where
The broken-winded, spavined stand
And crooked shopkeepers said that he
Might do a season on the land –
But not for high-paid work in towns.
He'd do a tinker, possibly.
I begged, 'O make some offer now,
A soul is a poor man's tragedy.
He'll draw your dungiest cart,' I said,
'Show you short cuts to Mass,
Teach weather lore, at night collect
Bad debts from poor men's grass.'
                    And they would not.

Where the
Tinkers quarrel I went down
With my horse, my soul.
I cried, 'Who will bid me half a crown?'
From their rowdy bargaining
Not one turned. 'Soul,' I prayed,
'I have hawked you through the world
Of Church and State and meanest trade.
But this evening, halter off,
Never again will it go on.
On the south side of ditches
There is grazing of the sun.
No more haggling with the world . . .'

As I said these words he grew
Wings upon his back. Now I may ride him
Every land my imagination knew.

Memory of Brother Michael

It would never be morning, always evening,
Golden sunset, golden age –
When Shakespeare, Marlowe and Jonson were writing
The future of England page by page,
A nettle-wild grave was Ireland's stage.

It would never be spring, always autumn,
After a harvest always lost,
When Drake was winning seas for England

We sailed in puddles of the past
Chasing the ghost of Brendan's mast.

The seeds among the dust were less than dust,
Dust we sought, decay,
The young sprout rising smothered in it,
Cursed for being in the way –
And the same is true today.

Culture is always something that was,
Something pedants can measure,
Skull of bard, thigh of chief,
Depth of dried-up river.
Shall we be thus for ever?
Shall we be thus for ever?

Bluebells for Love

There will be bluebells growing under the big trees
And you will be there and I will be there in May;
For some other reason we both will have to delay
The evening in Dunshaughlin – to please
Some imagined relation,
So both of us came to walk through that plantation.

We will be interested in the grass,
In an old bucket-hoop, in the ivy that weaves
Green incongruity among dead leaves,
We will put on surprise at carts that pass –

Only sometimes looking sideways at the bluebells in the
    plantation,
And never frighten them with too wild an exclamation.

We will be wise, we will not let them guess
That we are watching them or they will pose
A mere façade like boys
Caught out in virtue's naturalness.
We will not impose on the bluebells in that plantation
Too much of our desire's adulation.

We will have other loves – or so they'll think;
The primroses or the ferns or the briars,
Or even the rusty paling wires,
Or the violets on the sunless sorrel bank.
Only as an aside the bluebells in the plantation
Will mean a thing to our dark contemplation.

We'll know love little by little, glance by glance.
Ah, the clay under these roots is so brown!
We'll steal from Heaven while God is in the town –
I caught an angel smiling in a chance
Look through the tree-trunks of the plantation
As you and I walked slowly to the station.

Temptation in Harvest

A poplar leaf was spiked upon a thorn
Above the hedge like a flag of surrender
That the year hung out. I was afraid to wonder
At capitulation in a field of corn.
The yellow posies in the headland grass
Paraded up and down in loud apparel;
If I could search their hearts I'd find a moral
For men and women – but I let them pass.
Hope guarantees the poor that they will be
Masters at haw-time when the robins are
Courageous as a crow or water-hen. O see
There someone on an ash tree's limb
Sawing a stick for a post or a drilling-bar!
I wish that I this moment were with him!

I should not have wished, should not have seen how white
The wings of thistle seeds are, and how gay
Amoral Autumn gives her soul away
And every maidenhead without a fight.
I turned to the stubble of the oats,
Knowing that clay could still seduce my heart
After five years of pavements raised to art.
O the devilry of the fields! petals that goats
Have plucked from rose bushes of vanity!
But here! a small blue flower creeping over
On a trailing stem across an inch-wide chasm.
Even here wild gods have set a net for sanity.
Where can I look and not become a lover
Terrified at each recurring spasm?

This time of the year mind worried
About the threshing of the corn and whether
The yellow streaks in the sunset were for fine weather.
The sides of the ricks were letting in; too hurried
We built them to beat the showers that were flying
All day. 'It's raining in Drummeril now,'
We'd speculate, half happy to think how
Flat on the ground a neighbour's stooks were lying.
Each evening combing the ricks like a lover's hair,
Gently combing the butt-ends to run the rain,
Then running to the gate to see if there
Was anybody travelling on the train.
The Man in the Moon has water on the brain!
I love one! but my ricks are more my care.

An old woman whispered from a bush: 'Stand in
The shadow of the ricks until she passes;
You cannot eat what grows upon Parnassus –
And she is going there as sure as sin.'
I saw her turn her head as she went down
The blackberry lane-way, and I knew
In my heart that only what we love is true –
And not what loves us, we should make our own.
I stayed in indecision by the gate,
As Christ in Gethsemane, to guess
Into the morrow and the day after,
And tried to keep from thinking on the fate
Of those whom beauty tickles into laughter
And leaves them on their backs in muddiness.

The air was drugged with Egypt. Could I go
Over the field to the City of the Kings
Where art, music, letters are the real things?
The stones of the street, the sheds, hedges cried, No.

Earth, earth! I dragged my feet off the ground.
Labourers, animals armed with farm tools,
Ringed me. The one open gap had larch poles
Across it now by memory secured and bound.
The flaggers in the swamp were the reserves
Waiting to lift their dim nostalgic arms
The moment I would move. The noise of carts
Softening into haggards wove new charms.
The simplest memory plays upon the nerves
Symphonies that break down what the will asserts.

O Life, forgive me for my sins! I can hear
In the elm by the potato-pits a thrush;
Rain is falling on the Burning Bush
Where God appeared. Why now do I fear
That clear in the sky where the Evening Star is born?
Why does the inconsequential gabble
Of an old man among the hills so trouble
My thoughts this September evening? Now I turn
Away from the ricks, the sheds, the cabbage garden,
The stones of the street, the thrush song in the tree,
The potato-pits, the flaggers in the swamp;
From the country heart that hardly learned to harden,
From the spotlight of an old-fashioned kitchen lamp
I go to follow her who winked at me.

Father Mat

I

                    In a meadow
Beside the chapel three boys were playing football.
At the forge door an old man was leaning
Viewing a hunter-hoe. A man could hear
If he listened to the breeze the fall of wings –
How wistfully the sin-birds come home!

It was Confession Saturday, the first
Saturday in May; the May Devotions
Were spread like leaves to quieten
The excited armies of conscience.
The knife of penance fell so like a blade
Of grass that no one was afraid.

Father Mat came slowly walking, stopping to
Stare through gaps at ancient Ireland sweeping
In again with all its unbaptized beauty:
The calm evening,
The whitethorn blossoms,
The smell from ditches that were not Christian.
The dancer that dances in the hearts of men cried:
Look! I have shown this to you before –
The rags of living surprised,
The joy in things you cannot forget.

His heavy hat was square upon his head,
Like a Christian Brother's;
His eyes were an old man's watery eyes,
Out of his flat nose grew spiky hairs.

He was a part of the place,
Natural as a round stone in a grass field;
He could walk through a cattle fair
And the people would only notice his odd spirit there.

His curate passed on a bicycle –
He had the haughty intellectual look
Of the man who never reads in brook or book;
A man designed
To wear a mitre,
To sit on committees –
For will grows strongest in the emptiest mind.

The old priest saw him pass
And, seeing, saw
Himself a medieval ghost.
Ahead of him went Power,
One who was not afraid when the sun opened a flower,
Who was never astonished
At a stick carried down a stream
Or at the undying difference in the corner of a field.

II

The Holy Ghost descends
At random like the muse
On wise man and fool,
And why should poet in the twilight choose?

Within the dim chapel was the grey
Mumble of prayer
To the Queen of May –
The Virgin Mary with the schoolgirl air.

Two guttering candles on a brass shrine
Raised upon the wall
Monsters of despair
To terrify deep into the soul.

Through the open door the hum of rosaries
Came out and blended with the homing bees.
                    The trees
Heard nothing stranger than the rain or the wind
Or the birds –
But deep in their roots they knew a seed had sinned.

In the graveyard a goat was nibbling at a yew,
The cobbler's chickens with anxious looks
Were straggling home through nettles, over graves.
A young girl down a hill was driving cows
To a corner at the gable-end of a roofless house.

Cows were milked earlier,
The supper hurried,
Hens shut in,
Horses unyoked,
And three men shaving before the same mirror.

III

The trip of iron tips on tile
Hesitated up the middle aisle,
Heads that were bowed glanced up to see
Who could this last arrival be.

Murmur of women's voices from the porch,
Memories of relations in the graveyard.
On the stem
Of memory imaginations blossom.

In the dim
Corners in the side seats faces gather,
Lit up now and then by a guttering candle
And the ghost of day at the window.
A secret lover is saying
Three Hail Marys that she who knows
The ways of women will bring
Cathleen O'Hara (he names her) home to him.
Ironic fate! Cathleen herself is saying
Three Hail Marys to her who knows
The ways of men to bring
Somebody else home to her –
'O may he love me.'
What is the Virgin Mary now to do?

IV

From a confessional
The voice of Father Mat's absolving
Rises and falls like a briar in the breeze.
As the sins pour in the old priest is thinking
His fields of fresh grass, his horses, his cows,
His earth into the fires of Purgatory.
It cools his mind.
'They confess to the fields,' he mused,
'They confess to the fields and the air and the sky,'
And forgiveness was the soft grass of his meadow by the river;
His thoughts were walking through it now.

His human lips talked on:
'My son,
Only the poor in spirit shall wear the crown;
Those down

Can creep in the low door
On to Heaven's floor.'

The Tempter had another answer ready:
'Ah lad, upon the road of life
'Tis best to dance with Chance's wife
And let the rains that come in time
Erase the footprints of the crime.'

The dancer that dances in the hearts of men
Tempted him again:
'Look! I have shown you this before;
From this mountain-top I have tempted Christ
With what you see now
Of beauty – all that's music, poetry, art
In things you can touch every day.
I broke away
And rule all dominions that are rare;
I took with me all the answers to every prayer
That young men and girls pray for: love, happiness, riches –'
O Tempter! O Tempter!

V

As Father Mat walked home
Venus was in the western sky
And there were voices in the hedges:
'God the Gay is not the Wise.'

'Take your choice, take your choice,'
Called the breeze through the bridge's eye,
'The domestic Virgin and Her Child
Or Venus with her ecstasy.'

In Memory of My Mother

I do not think of you lying in the wet clay
Of a Monaghan graveyard; I see
You walking down a lane among the poplars
On your way to the station, or happily

Going to second Mass on a summer Sunday –
You meet me and you say:
'Don't forget to see about the cattle –'
Among your earthiest words the angels stray.

And I think of you walking along a headland
Of green oats in June,
So full of repose, so rich with life –
And I see us meeting at the end of a town

On a fair day by accident, after
The bargains are all made and we can walk
Together through the shops and stalls and markets
Free in the oriental streets of thought.

O you are not lying in the wet clay,
For it is a harvest evening now and we
Are piling up the ricks against the moonlight
And you smile up at us – eternally.

On Raglan Road

On Raglan Road on an autumn day I met her first and knew
That her dark hair would weave a snare that I might one day rue;
I saw the danger, yet I walked along the enchanted way,
And I said, let grief be a fallen leaf at the dawning of the day.

On Grafton Street in November we tripped lightly along the ledge
Of the deep ravine where can be seen the worth of passion's
    pledge,
The Queen of Hearts still making tarts and I not making hay –
O I loved too much and by such, by such, is happiness thrown
    away.

I gave her gifts of the mind, I gave her the secret sign that's known
To the artists who have known the true gods of sound and stone
And word and tint. I did not stint for I gave her poems to say
With her own name there and her own dark hair like clouds over
    fields of May.

On a quiet street where old ghosts meet I see her walking now
Away from me so hurriedly my reason must allow
That I had wooed not as I should a creature made of clay –
When the angel woos the clay he'd lose his wings at the dawn of
    day.

1947—55

Jim Larkin

Not with public words now can his greatness
Be told to the children, for he was more
Than a labour-agitating orator –
The flashing flaming sword merely bore witness
To the coming of the dawn. 'Awake and look!
The flowers are growing for you, and wonderful trees,
And beyond are not the serf's grey docks, but seas –
Excitement out of the creator's poetry book.
When the Full Moon's in the River the ghost of bread
Must not haunt all your weary wanderings home.
The ships that were dark galleys can become
Pine forests under the winter's starry plough
And the brown gantries will be the lifted hand
Of man the dreamer whom the gods endow.'
And thus I hear Jim Larkin shout above
The crowd who wanted to turn aside
From Reality coming to free them. Terrified,
They hid in the clouds of dope and would not move.
They ate the opium of the murderer's story
In the Sunday newspapers; they stood to stare
Not at a blackbird, but at a millionaire
Whose horses ran for serfdom's greater glory.
And Tyranny trampled them in Dublin's gutter,
Until Larkin came along and cried
The call of Freedom and the call of Pride,
And Slavery crept to its hands and knees,
And Nineteen Thirteen cheered from out the utter
Degradation of their miseries.

The Wake of the Books

A Mummery

Dramatis Personae (In the order of their appearance)

M.C. Master of Ceremonies	An Editor
Chorus (The Blue Hussars)	A Poet
Sean O'Faolain	Austin Clarke
First Millionaire	Second Millionaire
Patrick Kavanagh	An Actor
A Woman	An Actress
Frank O'Connor	An Alleged Film Director
An Old Priest	Young B.L.
A Young Priest	Young Solicitor
	Politician

Prologue
This little drama that I introduce
Is no great lecher to excite my muse,
For howsoever I try I can't but feel
The censorship of books is not a real
Problem for the writers of this land:
There's much that's insincere in what is banned –
And time if left the corpse would bury it deeper
In ten years than our bitterest conscience-keeper.

Yet, as I have been asked to undertake
Master of Ceremonies at this comic wake
As I lead the characters in I'll try
To show the kernel of the tragedy –
The reality of bank and bake-house
Screeching unheeded round the writer's wake-house,

The inarticulate envy and the spleen
Echoing in the incidental scene
We call the Censorship.

      But before
My mummers enter by the imaginary door,
I'd like to say a few words here –
(Not yet remove the draping from the bier).
Our greatest censors and worst enemies
Are those who gurgle praise – so soft to please.
The 'last judgment' that William Blake demanded
Would leave nine-tenths of these rhymesters stranded.

It all adds up to native cultural life,
The whore's honoured as the chastest wife;
The journalists cheer loudly for all,
The noblest verse and the stupidest doggerel.
      But I delay –
You did not come to hear me, but a play.

The scene you must imagine is a Square
Overlooked by windows, there and there and there!
In the centre is the corpse, a coffin filled
With all the books the censorship has killed.
Here all the streams of society converge –
New Rich, Old Rich, purple and navy-serge;
Bishops, priests, nuns; art patrons who
Would run a brothel if it paid them to.
These last I would particularly like to send
To hell at once, for these pretend
More than all others that a man can serve
Not two but twenty masters. You shall have
The ordinary people surging round
As you imagine.

Let the gong sound.
And now we bring the chorus in (some rousing airs)
And what better chorus than the Blue Hussars
Dressed for the show parade
And wearing yards of rich heraldic braid.
And what it symbolizes we don't know or care.
Now the Chorus gallops round the evening Square.

Chorus:
Horses, horses, horses, horses,
Cheer the hoof-marks of our race,
Horses, horses, horses, horses
Since Finn McCool have owned this place.
Horse-faced women, horse-faced men –
Horses, horses, horses, horses –
The horse is mightier than the pen.
The stick of evil stirs the sources
Of poetry and philosophy,
Muddies the pool, but road necks bend
Over true springs of gaiety.
Burn all books, let no more be penned.

O horses, horses, horses
Are the things to run in verses,
On the course or in the show ring,
Let us hear their noble snoring . . .

M.C.:
Now the Chorus goes and I shall call
Upon the servants to remove the pall.
That done I call on Sean O'Faolain's muse
To favour us with his peculiar views.

Sean O'Faolain:
When I and O'Connor sauntered by the Lee
In the silver springtime of our Gaelic dream,
We saw a people rising who did deem
The apotheosis of true liberty
To be the heart run wild in Nature's way –
Perhaps 'twas Munster we had in our minds –
We never thought that what frees also binds.
And I became the Hamlet of the play,
With yes and no and ifs and buts and maybes,
The philosophic doubt that has no centre –
But the certainty that centred our great mentor,
Filled his muse with poison worse than rabies.
Religion, is it false or is it true?
Can one go picking berries in the procession?
Can the artist's pride survive a good confession?
These are the questions I am putting to you.

M.C.:
This doesn't seem to make the play progress,
You're leading us into a wilderness.
I want to see you lost in angry sadness
About the judgment on *Midsummer Madness.*

Sean O'Faolain:
I wrote that book when I and O'Connor held
The fantasy of living warm in love;
There's faith in it and something born of
The intangible passion that has impelled
Young men to leave the cool paths of grass,
The luxury of April-furnished ditches,
To be seduced by desert-wandering witches
And walk barefoot on broken, poisonous glass.
O may I lift this poor child of mine

Out of the coffin for one last look –
Ah me! I never wrote a better book,
A little bit Chekhovian but – still fine.

M.C.:
I draw your attention to that window there,
The big bay window to the left of the Square,
Look straight I bid you with no artistic bias
And you will see three men wearing long pious
Faces; these three men are millionaires,
They dance, they race – and always say their prayers.
Come here my smiling friend,
A little nearer the window: there's one here
Of whom corrupt Power has need to fear,
Dead ideas that once shocked are in the pillory,
The writers are playing with their grandmothers' frillery.
Synge, Yeats, and yesterday, the fiddle-faddle
As futile as the heroes of the saddle.
Come, millionaires, and let the people hear
About your road of fortune –
Now give ear.

First Millionaire:
Money! Money!
Who measures success in money? I had imagined
That I was speaking to poets. Money! Money!
Money has no interest for me, my ideal
Is my country prosperous, my workers paid
Each Friday evening. Since the day I fought
In nineteen-sixteen I have had one thought:
Home industries, self-sufficiency, national fame.
I started as a poor man with an empty pocket
But with my ideal in my heart's gold locket.

Voice from the Back:
Shite.

First Millionaire (Pointing):
Master of Ceremonies, there's a group down there
Intriguing in that corner of the Square.

Patrick Kavanagh:
Prosperity's purse is a heart that's hollowed,
Virtue that's merely emptiness goes well
With bishops sometimes . . .

Hysterical Female Voices:
Anti-clerical! Anti-clerical!

M.C.:
Here enters from the big suburban houses
A well clad woman who stops where Kavanagh browses
Over the coffin where the condemned books lie;
She's sniffing for some spicy ribaldry.

Woman:
Forever Amber?

M.C.:
She pokes the bookish belly
Expecting what is bawdy to be smelly.

Kavanagh:
Madam, I have been a book reviewer;
You'll find the novel you seek in any sewer;
The novels in this literary coffin
Are merely truth that you would find most shocking.

Woman:
Here's Kate O'Brien's lovely *Land of Spices*
And *The Midnight Court* that nearly caused a crisis.
No wonder the library of the R.D.S.
Is such a frightfully boring wilderness.

M.C.:
That's enough of that. Who's next?
No, not O'Rahilly, he'd take Sterling as his text,
Nor Segrave-Daly who has apples on the brain.
Come Frank O'Connor, but please do refrain
From getting angry over culture here;
It's not much better in England now I fear.

Frank O'Connor:
I am not interested one way or the other
Whether they ban or unban; we do not matter.
We have put ourselves out of the world,
Eliminated ourselves.
The most immoral place of all
Is the middle of the road. Neutrality
Was our destruction.
I saw the little English girls working
In their pretty over-alls and I knew then
That this was life with all the enthusiasm
Of faith young in the world again.
(*Sneers from several windows*)
'Tis better to believe in something wrong
Than to be blasé, cynical as here,
Accepting every pious racketeer.
We live skin deep. We lack the courage
To lie close to life like the English.
Let them ban the books,
Let them ban the books.

You have your bishops and knights and rooks
And the pawns to be shifted about by crooks.
Haw, haw, I laugh at the silly tripe
As the dust of the town from my feet I wipe.
Banned or unbanned
I see no hope for this hopeless land.

An Old Priest:
He has the enthusiasm of a lover in pain,
No mind-frosted faith in that heart's rich vein.

A Young Priest:
If I had my way I'd never let him back,
I'd stretch him and all scribblers on the rack.
He writes of priests as sinners; would you not ban
The blackguardly works of such a man?

Old Priest:
God did not breed Pegasus for a halter,
In the fields of faith his gallop does not falter.

Young Priest:
He sneers at marriage, all these writers sneer
At the Sacrament of Matrimony here.

Old Priest:
Sneers!
In my parish for twenty years
There isn't a marriage to sneer at.
The old unmarried people sneer at life,
While every writer has at least one wife.
When I see the old maids
Coming along the country roads
To be confessed,
I hear the blasphemy of the foul beast.

Young Priest (*aside*):
Horrible old man,
Country living has degraded him:
Bulls and cows
And immoral cocks in the hen house.

M.C.:
An editor has been speaking, let us heed him
And then we will not need to read him.

An Editor:
We fought all censorships, tooth and nail,
We dared to print the Windsors' photos daily
And Princess Elizabeth's too.
We kept our Saturday poets going gaily.
We've got the reins of power now. The Taoiseach,
A man for whom I have the greatest *gradh*,
Is a decent man. But it remains to be seen
If the Gaelic child is worthy of the Da.

Jeering voices:
Blah, blah, blah!

M.C.:
It is about time to bring in the Chorus again,
A different Chorus this time.
Will some man come and look down the street at the mountains
And tell us what he feels?
A Poet! All in rags, indifferent to convention.

A Poet:
The leaves are falling on the suburban roads
And red flowers in a garden look tired,
And there is a mist like a sombre curtain on the Georgian façades,
And the laugh of the poor is life that has not tired.

I feel as I look that we are waiting for
A new and surprising world that is coming round the turn,
The first years of Christendom. There's the same air
And the same strange hope exciting a life-sick world.
That gay young girl of fashion has a smile
That is virtue under the cloak of coquetry
And she is faith and hope in what is real.
And she has scorn for the empty musketry
Of pleasure that means nothing called to grow.
She dances now but seems to keep forgetting
The glide that is vain. Dance finished, she will not bow.

Austin Clarke:
Derivative verse echoing the nineteenth century.

O'Connor:
Destructive critic, nothing survives his breath,
Greater enemy than the censorship.

Clarke:
Go back to the B.B.C.

M.C. (like a radio commentator):
Now round the corpse a brawl is taking place.
Poets, Essayists, Novelists, in-fight, embrace;
With light of battle in his schoolboy face
Smyllie is there making a ring for the row.
Clarke is taking the count. No, he is lifted now
By one of the MacManuses, I don't know which.
The millionaires from their windows look on
Filled with delight. O'Faolain takes no sides,
The Hamlet of the play is in two minds.
Now Smyllie rings a bell and thunders, 'Stop it,
Nemo me impune lacessit!'

The *Independent*'s writing a headline:
'Disgraceful scenes at a literary wake'.
Out of the confusion I now can see
Who's for life and who's for death.
Watch where the millionaires look smilingly.

A Second Millionaire:
'Tis wonderful to see the writers so free
From all convention. The only life that's beautiful
Is the poet's.
There are hundreds of poets in this city.

Clarke:
Many hundreds.

O'Connor:
Blasphemy.

Third Millionaire:
There are a few there whom I would never trust;
We'll have to prove them sinners or just mad.

First Millionaire:
No need. So long as we can keep the legend up
That there are hundreds of them, poets, writers,
We're safe. Let that be published in the press tomorrow
And plug the idea of milling geniuses
As common as dirt, the two-a-penny story.
The general bedlam will discredit all.
Off to the Scuttery now to collect our wives.

M.C.:
A group of actors has now arrived from the west
Bound for the Abbey and a film test.

An Actor:
Books! Such a lot of books. Who wrote all these?
Such trash! No *Captain Boycott* or *Green Years*.
Colum, I suppose. Those trampy men
Are writers? Very stupid-looking then.

An Actress:
My mother said to keep away from writers.
She said they beetened to be very good
Or they'd be taken up by Hollywood.

Kavanagh (To an actress):
Hello.

M.C.:
She turns away from Kavanagh's queer virility
With an upstart peasant's insultability.
And she speaks to one whom she takes for a film director
With a sigh, remembering her mother's 'God protect her.'

Alleged Film Director (To actress):
Come to my hotel. I want to give you an audition.
(*Sounds from the crowd.*)

M.C.:
Now cut the laughter! Poor Kavanagh's very sad
To lose such beauty to a brainless cad.
The Government Party arrives. My! How it swells
With young unemployed solicitors and B.L.s.

Young B.L. (To young solicitor):
I think there's fifteen more years in the Party,
In that case I'd be fixed before I'm forty;
A District Justiceship would not be bad
If there was nothing better to be had.

The law's the last, at present not a crumb in,
Although I am the chairman of my Cumann.
My father – blast his sowl, he worked instead
Of dying on the hills – he died in bed;
The bloody fool, he worked till old age got him
And so I have to climb from bed-rock bottom.

Young Solicitor:
My partner's gone to jail – embezzlement
Of moneys that were some old women's rent,
But I came free;
I hope it doesn't do me injury.
And I came here to join the howling mob
Of censors – it is one way to a job.

Young B.L.:
A simple tip, my friend, before we part –
Be seen at concerts and learn to talk of Art,
There's virtue in abstract painting – and Mozart.
But damn all native writers to perdition . . .
Silence! Here comes a noted politician.

Politician:
I love to see you literary boys
Raising our country in the world's eyes.

O'Faolain:
And yet you have the brazen cheek to ban us?

Politician:
What does it matter what I in private feel?
There's such a business as the public weal.

M.C.:
It seems to me another row is brewing.
Some nasty pens are busily reviewing
A book that tells of profits and of jobbery,
Government Gaelic screams: 'Ná h-abair é!'
The reviewer writes: 'These controversial matters
Are unworthy of the author's fine afflatus;
He lets us down in public . . .'
So in case
Further brawlings should our dead disgrace
We'll call in our poet to relieve
With the light of his imagination this make-believe.

Poet:
Sometimes I can see in these poor streets
A little village, and hear in the women's gossip
The talk of country women at a well
Echoing in the valleys.
The women selling oranges have a grip
On life that our Censorship
Would call obscene –
Life pressed in the gutter yields the gutter's dream
Of flowers.
I have no fear, new Aprils will be ours.

I see young boys climbing a wall,
And little girls playing with a doll.
Hell battles with heaven for every inch of ground,
Yet nowhere do I see God losing a round.

And I know that poetry will never lose its courage,
That men will always be moved to happiness
By the sun rising or the sun setting or the brown ivy,
Or the wild swing of a young man in love

Going down the stone steps from his girl's hall door.
Let it be an October stubble field or a cluster of grey gables
Upon which the moonlight falls, our gasp will be the same
For something remembered, some intensity
Of clay transfigured in an innocent dream.

When I look down the river at the painted houses
And gaze in old alleyways, I hear
The girl of the eighteenth century singing
'Cockles and Mussels', and I have no fear
For what is beautiful. The song will continue
And the children of the gods whose hearts are humble
Will hear, will hear.

M.C.:
They're taking the coffin up. They're moving away.
Ah, the writers too are living in yesterday,
Challenging the enemy that died last night,
For the spirit in travail now they have no sight
To see or ears to hear, or words to name
The lies that crowd around this day's life-dream.
Synge who drove people wild is now the vogue . . .
But I must give way to the

Epilogue
The wake is over now and my drama
Resolved itself into a panorama.
The curtain woven from the passing day
Showed up the futile shadows of the play.
And showed up also I sincerely trust
Spirits who fertilize the world's dust.

Jungle

Through the jungle of Pembroke Road
I have dragged myself in terror,
Listening to the lions of Frustration roar:
The anguish of beasts that have had their dinner
And found there was something inside
Gnawing away unsatisfied.

As far as Ballsbridge I walked in wonder,
Down Clyde to Waterloo,
Watching the natives pulling the jungle
Grass of Convention to cover the nude
Barbaric buttocks where tail-stumps showed
When Reason lit up the road.

On Baggot Street Bridge they screeched,
Then dived out of my sight
Into the pools of blackest porter –
Till half-past ten of the jungle night
The bubbles came up with toxic smell
From Frustration's holy well.

No Social Conscience

He was an egoist with an unsocial conscience,
And I liked him for it though he was out of favour,
For he seemed to me to be sincere,
Wanting to be no one's but his own saviour.

He saw the wild eyes that are the Public's
Turned on the one man who held
Against the gangs of fear his ordinary soul –
He did no public service but lived for himself.

His one enthusiasm was against the hysteria,
Those dangerous men who are always in procession
Searching for someone to murder or worship –
He never qualified for a directorship or a State pension.

The Paddiad

or: The Devil as a Patron of Irish Letters

In the corner of a Dublin pub
This party opens – blub-a-blub –
Paddy Whiskey, Rum and Gin,
Paddy Three Sheets in the Wind,
Paddy of the Celtic Mist,
Paddy Connemara West,

Chestertonian Paddy Frog
Croaking nightly in the bog.
All the Paddies having fun
Since Yeats handed in his gun.
Every man completely blind
To the truth about his mind.

In their middle sits a fellow
Aged about sixty, bland and mellow;
Saintly silver locks of hair,
Quiet-voiced as monk at prayer;
Every Paddy's eye is glazed
On this fellow. Mouths amazed
Drink in all his words of praise.
O comic muse descend to see
The devil Mediocrity,
For that is the devil sitting there,
Actually Lucifer.

He has written many Catholic novels,
None of which mention devils:
Daring men, beautiful women,
Nothing about muck or midden,
Wholesome atmosphere – Why must
So-called artists deal with lust?

About the devil's dark intentions
There are some serious misconceptions:
The devil is supposed to be
A nasty man entirely,
Horned and hoofed and fearful gory –
That's his own invented story.

The truth in fact is the reverse
He does not know a single curse;
His forte's praise for what is dead,
Pegasus Munnings bred.
Far and near he screws his eyes
In search of what will never rise,
Souls that are fusty, safe and dim,
These are the geniuses of the land to him.

Most generous-tempered of the gods
He listens to the vilest odes,
Aye, and not just idle praise!
For these the devil highly pays.
And the crowds for culture cheer and cheer:
'A modern Medici is here,
Never more can it be said
That Irish poets are not fed.'
The boys go wild and toast the Joker,
The master of the mediocre.

'A great renaissance is under way'
You can hear the devil say
As into our pub comes a new arrival,
A man who looks the conventional devil:
This is Paddy Conscience, this
Is Stephen Dedalus,
This is Yeats who ranted to
Knave and fool before he knew,
This is Sean O'Casey saying,
Fare thee well to Inishfallen.

He stands on the perimeter of the crowd
Half drunk to show that he's not proud
But willing given half a chance
To play the game with any dunce;

He wears a beaten bedraggled pose
To put the devil at his ease,
But Lucifer sees through the pose
Of drunken talk and dirty clothes;
The casual word that drops by chance
Denotes a dangerous arrogance,
Still sober and alive enough
To blast this world with a puff.

Every Paddy sitting there
Pops up like a startled hare,
Loud ignorings fill each face –
This behaviour's a disgrace,
A savage intruding on our Monday's
Colloquy on trochees, spondees,
And whether Paddy Mist or Frog
Is the greatest singer of the bog.
Hypodermics sourpiss loaded
Are squirted at our foolish poet.
The devil sips his glass of plain
And takes up his theme again:

'My suggestion is for a large bounty
For the best poet in each county.
How many poems, Mist, can you spare
For my new anthology of Clare?
Ten guineas per poem is fair,
But they must definitely be Clare;
Some lyrics in your recent volume
Were influenced by Roscommon.'

Conscience: 'I'm a Clareman more than Mist.'
Mist: 'But essentially a novelist.'
Frog: 'Essentially a man of prose
As any whole-time verseman knows.

I think that Paddy Connemara West
Is worth twenty guineas at least.'
'I agree, Frog,
West is one of the great singers of the bog –
I'll give him twenty guineas, so –'

'Oh, oh, oh,'
Conscience is going mad,
Tearing, raving, using bad
Language in the bar
Where the bards of Ireland are.
Now peace again, they've chucked him out.
Paddy Frog puts down his stout,
Clenches his chubby grocer's fist,
Says: 'I disagree with Mist
That Paddy Connemara West

Is inferior to Stephens at his best –
A Catholic and Gaelic poet,
His last group of poems show it.'
Devil: 'Paddy Connemara gets my vote
As the expresser of the Catholic note.
His pious feeling for the body
And rejection of the shoddy
Mystical cloak that Conscience trails
Places him among the greatest of Gaels;
In my last radio talk I drew
Attention to this Froggish view.

We must bring out a Collected Edition
The money's a minor consideration –
What most we want to bring success
Is an end to petty bitterness,
No more slashing notices in the press

But something broadly generous.
We want an openness of heart –
No Olympian critic saying: depart
From me ye cursed pack of fools,
Only poetasters form schools.
You remember Paddy Conscience:
"Count me out at Mummers' rantings." '

Here news has just come in that Paddy
Conscience lost his latest body,
Dead in Paris –
The devil sighs – 'Shocking news.
I much admired all his views.
A man of genius, generous, kind,
Not a destructive idea in his mind.
My dearest friend! Let's do him proud.
Our wives will make a green silk shroud
To weave him in. The Emerald Isle
Must bury him in tourist style.

A broadcast on his work might be,
A reading of his poetry.
The Government will give a grant
To build a worthy monument,
I know the Minister involved,
The cost will readily be halved.
Before we part let's make a date
To meet tomorrow night at eight
To make the final funeral plans,
For this will be Ireland seen by France.
This is the window of our shop.
Paddy Mist might do an ap-
Preciation on the general
Culture of an Irish funeral.'

All the Paddies rise and hurry
Home to write the inside story
Of their friendship for the late
Genius who was surely great;
Recall his technical innovations,
His domestic life, his patience
With the humblest aspirant
On the literary bent.

All his hunger was imagined,
Never was a falser legend,
He could make whenever he chose
A fortune out of verse or prose.
Irish women spirituelles
Ran from race-tracks at his spell,
Left the beds of jockeys, actors –
These may be considered factors.

The group's dispersed. The devil stays,
Some discontent in his face.
Already he can see another
Conscience coming on to bother
Ireland with muck and anger,
Ready again to die of hunger,
Condemnatory and uncivil –
What a future for a devil!

Spring Day

O Come all ye tragic poets and sing a stave with me –
Give over T. S. Eliot and also W. B.
We'll sing our way through Stephen's Green where March has
    never found
In the growing grass a cadence of the verse of Ezra Pound.

The University girls are like tulip bulbs behind,
More luxurious than ever from Holland was consigned,
Those bulbs will shortly break in flower – rayon, silk and cotton –
And our verbal constipation will be totally forgotten.

Philosophy's a graveyard – only dead men analyse
The reason for existence. Come all you solemn boys
From out your dictionary world and literary gloom –
Kafka's mad, Picasso's sad in Despair's confining room.

O Come all darling poets and try to look more happy,
Forget about sexology as you gossip in the café;
Forget about the books you've read and the inbred verses there,
Forget about the Kinsey Report and take a mouthful of air.

The world began this morning, God-dreamt and full of birds,
The fashion shops were glorious with the new collection of words,
And Love was practising phrases in young balladry –
Ten thousand years must pass before the birth of Psychology.

O Come all ye gallant poets – to know it doesn't matter
Is Imagination's message – break out but do not scatter.
Ordinary things wear lovely wings – the peacock's body's
    common.
O Come all ye youthful poets and try to be more human.

Leave Them Alone

There's nothing happening that you hate
That's really worthwhile slamming;
Be patient. If you only wait
You'll see time gently damning

Newspaper bedlamites who raised
Each day the devil's howl,
Versifiers who had seized
The poet's begging bowl.

The whole hysterical passing show
The hour apotheosized
Into a cul-de-sac will go
And be not even despised.

Adventure in the Bohemian Jungle

A simple man arrived in town,
Lover of letters; more than that
A true believer in the mystical
Power of poets. Moral, yet
Willing for a well-made song
To let the poet choose his own.

The fruit would justify the rape
Of blossoms, though he might regret
The virgin pink of May –
And thus he came to get
A peep into the temple of
The Muses. He was full of love.

A bearded man who wore a cloak
He sighted. To himself, he said,
This is my man. He introduced
His plan. The bearded man replied,
I'll lead you through the world of art
Where beats a universal heart.

SCENE:

This is the entrance to the bohemian jungle which lies on the perimeter of Commerce.

From the depths of the rotten vegetation can be heard the screams of drunken girls.

The gabble from Schools of Acting, Painting, Music.

A stream of large cars passes in.

In one of these cars sits Count O'Mulligan, wealthy father of Sheila O'Mulligan, the star of *Cardinal Error.*

Count O'Mulligan brings with him two gross of gold, diamond-studded replicas of the Ardagh Chalice as cups to be competed for at the Drama Festival.

Above the stinking weeds, whose life is derived from the moonlight, rises the phallic tower of Bohemia's temple, The Theatre.

The Catholic Cultural League in procession headed by its Chaplain, Father John, who is loaded down with two gross of rosary beads for presentation to the performers, moves slowly through.

The fantasy reminds the Countryman of the nighttown scene in *Ulysses,* or Dante's Hell or something out of John Bunyan.

Through the railings is visible an apartment in which a wild bottle party is in progress. Young women are being led from the main room into bedrooms. One of these girls the Countryman recognises as the highly – as he imagined – respectable daughter of a highly respectable doctor.

In the foyers of several theatres can be seen a number of early middle-aged women who are talking about actors and musicians while trying to sow a catch-crop of passion in this favourable climate.

Other sights are: politicians carrying flags, the women correspondents of several newspapers, radio commentators, the President of the Travel Society. This man is showing some Americans around and explaining to them that Necessity Number One is not unavailable in this country. Snatches of the conversation come over:

American:
If there's no Sex, what good is my shillelagh?

Travelman:
The situation is improving daily.

Guide:
Here's where we go in –
Throw it away, throw it away, throw it away.

Countryman:
Throw what away?

Guide:
The cold disgust upon your face,
The Ussherine Refusal,
The cut-and-dried opinions –
See life as just amusing.

See life as newspapers show it
Without a moral judgement,

The bank Integrity
Holds but a beggar's lodgement.

Truth's what's in power to-day,
The lie's what's in the breadline,
So take your Gospel straight
From the morning headline.

Bow down to fools in office,
Keep yourself in practice,
Admire the successful,
But damn the beaten rackets.

Anticipate the failure,
His smile when out of place
Can blast your life. Have no
Memory for Failure's face.

Simply reverse the manner
By which you've lived till now;
Life is not a heifer
But a great-uddered cow.

They join the bottle-party where there is a constant shuffling and
poking of heads through the crowd as if everyone wanted to speak
to someone else.

Countryman:
Show me some authors.

Guide:
You saw the look they gave you, that was you
Being their conscience.
Hide that mirror.
Have a drink.

(*To barman*) Mick,
A ball.
(*To a man*) How is Des?

Countryman:
You know them all.
Have I to go through all this to find
The world of Art?

Guide:
For success, yes.
They will not accept
The man not broken and remade
To the formula.
The real is too unpredictable.
Have another drink . . .
Mick!

Countryman:
This is a wonderful world.
(*To a girl half-tight*)
How about me kissing you?

Before he has time to organise his courage there is a commotion near the door as the crowd rushes forward to catch a glimpse as Father John, Chaplain to the C.C.L., passes by with Sheila O'Mulligan on his arm.

Guide:
She's the Adjudicator at the Festival.

Countryman:
She looks a good thing.
There's something to be said for the common bitch,

She has not virtue's jealous-gripping power
Such
As the good woman who can devour
A man's mind and entrails, spit
His chewed-up personality out on to the grass
While her hungry thought goes screaming, howling wildly
For a soul, a soul to fill a gaping space.
For here is the stuffed tiger of Desire
With nylon fur and wire-recorded roar,
The flashing fangs like Instinct's, yet quite safe,
Quite safe . . .
And what a bore!

Angry faces are turned in the speaker's direction. A young man, with a frustrated grin, seizes the Countryman by the shoulder.

The Man:
Sheila's a very great artist,
Her performance in *Cardinal Error* was aesthetic.
The *Catholic World* by its readers' vote
Acclaimed her outstanding Catholic of the year . . .
So if you want your dial defaced –

Guide returns and explains that Countryman is a friend of his.

Countryman:
A thug!

Girl (whom he had tried to kiss):
Well, Jack's a friend of mine. See?
Come on, Jack, the curtain's going up;
Mummie's too tight to leave the (appropriate word) car.
Who was that bullock in the china-shop?

The Guide leads the Countryman out to get sick. Around them they see bodies in varying states of futile lechery. The President of the Travel Society and the American are judging a Beauty Competition. A woman reporter is present eagerly listening.

Travelman:
How do girls here compare . . . ?

The Guide and the Countryman move away to where Count O'Mulligan is standing talking to Father John.

Father John:
This is the great Art patron, Count O'Mulligan,
Sheila's father, the motor salesman.
Who's your friend?

Guide:
A man from the mythical land of Simple Country
Learning about life, about Art.

Chaplain:
Has he a grudge against life?
Why is he so sour?

Guide:
He is difficult, he sees life as morning in a field of dewy grass.
He is shocked at the corruption through which all must pass
To arrive at knowledge.
He will not take the world as it runs.
I fear he will suffer for his denial
Of what Is.

Guide follows Countryman who has moved away.

Guide:
Why did you insult the great O'Mulligan?
Richest man in town, worth knowing.

Countryman:
I know him;
He once employed a poet in his factory
At thirty bob a week
And gave ten thousand pounds to the C.C.L.
He has never committed rape or bigamy it is true,
Goes to Mass every morning in fact,
A good beginning to the businessman's day,
God nicely in His place, card-indexed,
His stomach comfortable on golf dreams,
The Bishop calling round to have dinner to discuss
With him the problem of the city's poor.
A charitable man is Count O'Mulligan,
Chairman of the Christian Beggars' Guild,
Benign, bountiful – evil.

There is further commotion as the Players made up for the verse-play pass by.

Countryman (*musingly*):
Sorcerers,
Medieval monks,
Ancient Abbesses,
Necromancers,
Alchemists.

Guide:
Culture on the march, join in.
Oh, here's the Count again.
Be nice to him.

The Count:
The greatest of the Arts is music –
Mozart, Beethoven, Kreisler, Menuhin;
After music, the art of the actor –
Olivier, Crosbie, Barry, Ireland's droll –

Chaplain:
And McCormick, Ireland's soul.

Newspaper photographers push Guide and Countryman aside to get shots of the Count and Father John. They interview Sheila O'Mulligan.

Interviewers:
What's your opinion of the atomic bomb?
Should it be outlawed by the United Nations?
What is the future of the film industry?
Will Television pay still higher wages?
What's your opinion of the American Theatre?
Who is America's outstanding mind?
What is your message to the Irish people?
Are we still the spiritual leaders of mankind?
Is religion still the force in Filmland?
Did the Cleaner Films and Rosary Crusade
Bring further customers to the Cinema?

Countryman:
O God! O God! O God!

Guide:
This is the world of Art,
Of Love.
You dream of romantic sin, the Seven
Are the locked doors of the idealistic Heaven.

Countryman:
I dreamt of sin and it was fire,
A May-time-in-the-fields desire,
Violent, exciting, new,
Whin-blossoms burning up the dew;
Sudden death and sudden birth
Among the hierarchies of the earth;
Kings that ruled with absolute power
If 'twas only for an hour;
Trees were green, mountains sheer
And God dramatically clear.
But here in this nondescript land
Everything is secondhand:
Nothing ardently growing,
Nothing coming, nothing going,
Tepid fevers, nothing hot,
None alive enough to rot;
Nothing clearly defined . . .
Every head is challenged. Friend,
This is hell you've brought me to.
Where's the gate that we came through?

Guide:
Simply imagine the nightmare's ended,
And you're already outside the gate
Watching the patrons, players, playboys
Worshipping the second-rate.
That's Hell's secret, to be the mirror
For a mixture of truth and error.

At this point the satire explodes in a burst of wild cheering as the
Countryman joins a group of Crumlin gurriers who are betting on a
competition for who can urinate the highest. The Countryman wins,
but is later arrested and charged with committing a public nuisance.

Ante-natal Dream

I only know that I was there
With hayseed in my hair
Lying on the shady side
Of a haycock in July.

A crowd was pressing round
My body on the ground,
Prising the lids of my eyes –
Open and you'll be wise.

The sky that roared with bees,
The row of poplar trees
Along the stream struck deep
And would not let me sleep.

A boortree tried hard to
Let me see it grow,
Mere notice was enough,
She would take care of love.

A clump of nettles cried:
We'll saturate your pride
Till you are oozing with
The richness of our myth.

For we are all you'll know
No matter where you go –
Every insect, weed,
Kept singing in my head.

Thistle, ragwort, bluebottle,
Cleg that maddens cattle
Were crowding round me there
With hayseed in my hair.

Bank Holiday

Nineteen-fifty was the year,
The August Bank Holiday that I was here,
Sitting in my room alone,
Conscious of a season gone;

Ultimate failure straggling up
Through the barren daydream crop.
I must not defer the date
For a meeting with my fate.

There he comes your alter ego
Past the Waterloo and Searson's
With a silly gaping mouth
Sucking smiles from every slut,
Sure that this is Heaven's high manna –
God is good to Patrick Kavanagh,
Building like a rejected lover
Dust into an ivory tower.

In the pubs for seven years
Men have given him their ears,
Buying the essence of his heart
With a porter-perfumed fart.

Make him turn his pockets out
And his seven harvests count.
Spread out the vain collection –
Not a ha'penny of affection.

Knock him to the ground for he
Is your sister Vanity,
Is your brother Clown
Exhibited for a sneering town.
He's your son who's named Tomorrow,
Kill him, kill Remorse, your mother,
Be the father of your fate
On this nineteen-fifty date.

Irish Poets Open Your Eyes

Irish poets open your eyes,
Even Cabra can surprise;
Try the dog-tracks now and then –
Shelbourne Park and crooked men.

Could you ever pray at all
In the Pro-Cathedral
Till a breath of simpleness
Freed your Freudian distress?

Enter in and be a part
Of the world's frustrated heart,
Drive the golf ball of despair,
Superdance away your care.

Be ordinary,
Be saving up to marry.
Kiss her in the alleyway,
Part – 'Same time, same place' – and go.

Learn repose on Boredom's bed,
Deep, anonymous, unread,
And the god of Literature
Will touch a moment to endure.

Tale of Two Cities

The streets of London are not paved with gold,
The streets of London are paved with failures;
They get up and move about when they are filled with drink,
Just as in Dublin. Yesterday in Fleet Street
In a pub I met one. He shook my hand
And he was full of poisonous good fellowship as he looked into
     my eyes:
I would have a double whiskey.
I was from Dublin, most wonderful spot on earth.

How was Harry Kelly, Jack Sullivan and Brady,
And Galligan, the greatest Dubliner of them all?
I'll tell you the name of the greatest living poet, he muttered,
He lives near Manchester and will be heard of yet.
What about Auden? I interrupted. He ignored me –
Yeats was second-rate, not a patch on Higgins –
I was back in Dublin as I listened.

You certainly must have another double whiskey, he cried
With tears of patriotism in his eyes,
And once again he gripped my hand in his
And said there was no place like Dublin.
His friendship wounded, but I dare not complain,
For that would seem boorish. Yet it was this
Insincere good-nature that hurt me in Dublin.
The sardonic humour of a man about to be hanged.
But London would not hang him; it laid him horizontal
To dream of the books he had written in liquor.
Once again he would return to Dublin
Where among the failures he would pass unnoticed,
Happy in pubs talking about yesterday's wits,
And George Moore's use of the semi-colon.

To Be Dead

To be dead is to stop believing in
The masterpieces we will begin tomorrow;
To be an exile is to be a coward,
To know that growth has stopped,
That whatever is done is the end;
Correct the proofs over and over,
Rewrite old poems again and again,
Tell lies to yourself about your achievement:
Ten printed books on the shelves.
Though you know that no one loves you for
What you have done,
But for what you might do.

And you perhaps take up religion bitterly
Which you laughed at in your youth,
Well, not actually laughed,
But it wasn't your kind of truth.

Kerr's Ass

We borrowed the loan of Kerr's big ass
To go to Dundalk with butter,
Brought him home the evening before the market
An exile that night in Mucker.

We heeled up the cart before the door,
We took the harness inside –
The straw-stuffed straddle, the broken breeching
With bits of bull-wire tied;

The winkers that had no choke-band,
The collar and the reins . . .
In Ealing Broadway, London Town,
I name their several names

Until a world comes to life –
Morning, the silent bog,
And the god of imagination waking
In a Mucker fog.

The Defeated

Always in pubs I meet them, the defeated,
With a long sweep of the face crying:
Ridiculous the idea that you have stated –
I lived ten years in that city, and you are lying
To say that houses with slate roofs exist,
With windows, wooden floors and rooms upstairs;
A dream, dear friend, there's no bed gives such rest
As a straw bed evenly spread. There are no powers
Greater than this most ancient barnyard knows.
And you'll come back, come back, come back –
They always do – in ten years or a score
And find this pig-sty for your pig's broad back,
And in it all religion, literature, art –
I know, I know the secret of your heart.

Drink up, drink up, the troughs in Paris and
London are no better than your own,
Joyce learned that bitterly in a foreign land.
Don't laugh, there is no answer to that one!
Outside this pig-sty life deteriorates,
Civilisation dwindles. We are the last preserve
Of Eden in a world of savage states.
With a touch more cunning and a touch more nerve
You'd establish at the trough your own good place;
Meet all the finest sows if you would just
Not damn each hog you meet straight to his face;
They're all your friends if you but knew. Please put
Your skyward-turned snout unto the ground
And nuts that Africa never knew you'll find.

Remember Colum and his fair-green promise,
Young maidens' laughter on a Midland lane,
A greater singer far than Dylan Thomas,
Phrase-maker innocent as April rain.
And see O'Casey lost in English Devon,
Who never wrote another line worth reading
Since he left St George's Pocket in 'twenty-seven,
Weaving in vain an alien material.
The blue and rapturous phrase, the brave banner
Of a man's own people shabby and torn,
Strained on the thorn of the English manner.
Lost is the man who thinks that he can scorn
His parish mother's paps. The greatest sage
May not reject his people's heritage.

Around you, don't forget is genius which
Walks with feet rooted in the native soil.
Don't sweep them from your path or say that such
Are merely drunken talkers without mind.
The poet's task is not to solve the riddle
Of Man and God but buckleap on a door
And grab his screeching female by her middle
To the music of a melodion (preferably), roar
Against the Western waves of Connemara,
Up lads and thrash the beetles. This tradition
Is what the stranger comes to buy or borrow,
What you would leave to chase a worthless mission.
Leave Christ and Christlike problems and you'll be
The synthesis of Gaelic poetry.

I went away and thought of all the answers,
But there were none that killed his ghastly smile
Which said to me: life has no enchantment,
Art is no more than Sancho Panza's Isle;

A phrase made up to crown a pint of beer,
A paragraph for a gossip columnist,
A group of idle men and women or
Anything temporary, sensationalist –
Shakespeare and Blake, where are they now, or Keats?
Drink up your drink, get yourself a job . . .
O God, I cried, these treats are not the treats
That Heaven offers in the Golden Cup.
And I heard the demon's terrifying yell:
There is no place as perfect as our hell.

Who Killed James Joyce?

Who killed James Joyce?
I, said the commentator,
I killed James Joyce
For my graduation.

What weapon was used
To slay mighty Ulysses?
The weapon that was used
Was a Harvard thesis.

How did you bury Joyce?
In a broadcast Symposium,
That's how we buried Joyce
To a tuneful encomium.

Who carried the coffin out?
Six Dublin codgers
Led into Langham Place
By W. R. Rodgers.

Who said the burial prayers? –
Please do not hurt me –
Joyce was no Protestant,
Surely not Bertie?

Who killed Finnegan?
I, said a Yale-man,
I was the man who made
The corpse for the wake man.

And did you get high marks,
The Ph.D.?
I got the B.Litt.
And my master's degree.

Did you get money
For your Joycean knowledge?
I got a scholarship
To Trinity College.

I made the pilgrimage
In the Bloomsday swelter
From the Martello Tower
To the cabby's shelter.

Portrait of the Artist

I never lived, I have no history,
I deserted no wife to take another,
I rotted in a room and leave – this message.

The morning newspapers and the radio
Announced his death in a few horrid words:
– A man of talent who lacked the little more
That makes the difference
Between success and failure.
The biographer turned away disgusted from
A theme that had no plot
And wrote instead the life of Reilly.

Great artist, came to town at twenty-one,
Took a job,
Threw it up,
Lived a year with Mrs Brown.

Wrote a play,
Got the pox,
Made a film,
Wrote the incidental music.

Left his Mrs.
Took another,
Lived in Paris
With a mummer.

His critics were
Denounced as monsters,
Jungle beasts
Who hated Art.

Great artist, great man, the pattern was perfect
And the biographer recorded it with enthusiasm.

Auditors In

I

The problem that confronts me here
Is to be eloquent yet sincere;
Let myself rip and not go phoney
In an inflated testimony.
Is verse an entertainment only?
Or is it a profound and holy
Faith that cries the inner history
Of the failure of man's mission?
Should it be my job to mention
Precisely how I chanced to fail
Through a cursed ideal?
Write down here: he knew what he wanted –
Evilest knowledge ever haunted
Man when he can picture clear
Just what he is searching for.

A car, a big suburban house,
Half secret that he might not lose
The wild attraction of the poor
But proud, the fanatic lure
For women of the poet's way
And diabolic underlay;
The gun of pride can bring them down
At twenty paces in the town –
For what? the tragedy is this:
Pride's gunman hesitates to kiss.

A romantic Rasputin
Praying at the heart of sin.
He cannot differentiate,
Say if he does not want to take
From moral motives or because
Nature has ideal in her laws.

But to get down to the factual –
You are not homosexual.
And yet you live without a wife,
A most disorganized sort of life.
You've not even bred illegitimates –
A lonely lecher whom the fates
By a financial trick castrate.

You're capable of an intense
Love that is experience.
Remember how your heart was moved
And youth's eternity was proved
When you saw a young girl going to Mass
On a weekday morning as
You yourself used to go
Down to church from Ednamo.

Your imagination still enthuses
Over the dandelions at Willie Hughes's
And these are equally valid
For urban epic, peasant ballad.
Not mere memory but the Real
Poised in the poet's commonweal.
And you must take yourself in hand
And dig and ditch your authentic land.

Wake up, wake up and compromise
On the non-essential sides.
Love's round you in a rapturous bevy
But you are bankrupt by the levy
Imposed upon the ideal:
Her Cheshire-cat smile surmounts the wall.
She smiles 'Wolf, wolf, come be my lover',
Unreal you find and yet you never
Catch on. One cannot but feel sorry,
For the ideal is purgatory.
Yet do not be too much dismayed;
It's on your hand the humble trade
Of versing that can easily
Restore your equanimity
And lay the looney ghosts that goad
The savages of Pembroke Road . . .
Bow down here and thank your God.

II

After the prayer I am ready to enter my heart,
Indifferent to the props of a reputation:
Some feeble sallies of a peasant plantation,
The rotten shafts of a remembered cart
Holding up the conscious crust of art.

No quiet corner here for contemplation,
No roots of faith to give my angry passion
Validity. I at the bottom will start,
Try to ignore the shame-reflecting eyes
Of worshippers who made their god too tall
To share their food or do the non-stupendous;
They gave him for exploring empty skies
Instead of a little room where he might write for
Men too real to live by vapid legends.

Away, away on wings like Joyce's,
Mother Earth is putting my brand new clothes in order,
Praying, she says, that I no more ignore her;
Yellow buttons she found in fields at bargain prices,
Kelly's Big Bush for a button-hole. Surprises
In every pocket – the stream at Connolly's corner,
Myself at Annavackey on the Armagh border,
Or calm and collected in a calving crisis.
Not sad at all as I float away, away,
With Mother keeping me to the vernacular.
I have a home to return to now. O blessing
For the return in Departure. Somewhere to stay
Doesn't matter. What is distressing
Is waking eagerly to go nowhere in particular.

From the sour soil of a town where all roots canker
I turn away to where the Self reposes,
The placeless Heaven that's under all our noses,
Where we're shut off from all the barren anger,
No time for self-pitying melodrama,
A million Instincts know no other uses
Than all day long to feed and charm the Muses
Till they become pure positive. O hunger,
Where all have mouths of desire and none

Is willing to be eaten! I am so glad
To come so accidentally upon
My Self at the end of a tortuous road
And have learned with surprise that God
Unworshipped withers to the Futile One.

Innocence

They laughed at one I loved –
The triangular hill that hung
Under the Big Forth. They said
That I was bounded by the whitethorn hedges
Of the little farm and did not know the world.
But I knew that love's doorway to life
Is the same doorway everywhere.

Ashamed of what I loved
I flung her from me and called her a ditch
Although she was smiling at me with violets.

But now I am back in her briary arms;
The dew of an Indian Summer morning lies
On bleached potato-stalks –
What age am I?

I do not know what age I am,
I am no mortal age;
I know nothing of women,
Nothing of cities,
I cannot die
Unless I walk outside these whitethorn hedges.

Epic

I have lived in important places, times
When great events were decided: who owned
That half a rood of rock, a no-man's land
Surrounded by our pitchfork-armed claims.
I heard the Duffys shouting 'Damn your soul'
And old McCabe, stripped to the waist, seen
Step the plot defying blue cast-steel –
'Here is the march along these iron stones'.
That was the year of the Munich bother. Which
Was most important? I inclined
To lose my faith in Ballyrush and Gortin
Till Homer's ghost came whispering to my mind.
He said: I made the *Iliad* from such
A local row. Gods make their own importance.

On Looking into E. V. Rieu's Homer

Like Achilles you had a goddess for mother,
For only the half-god can see
The immortal in things mortal;
The far-frightened surprise in a crow's flight,
Or the moonlight
That stays for ever in a tree.

In stubble fields the ghosts of corn are
The important spirits the imagination heeds.
Nothing dies; there are no empty
Spaces in the cleanest-reaped fields.

It was no human weakness when you flung
Your body prostrate on a cabbage drill –
Heart-broken with Priam for Hector ravaged;
You did not know why you cried,
This was the night he died –
Most wonderful-horrible
October evening among those cabbages.

The intensity that radiated from
The Far Field Rock – you afterwards denied –
Was the half-god seeing his half-brothers
Joking on the fabulous mountain-side.

God in Woman

Now I must search till I have found my God –
Not in an orphanage. He hides
In no humanitarian disguise,
A derelict upon a barren bog;
But in some fantastically ordinary incog:
Behind a well-bred convent girl's eyes,
Or wrapped in middle-class felicities
Among the women in a coffee shop.
Surely my God is feminine, for Heaven

Is the generous impulse, is contented
With feeding praise to the good. And all
Of these that I have known have come from women.
While men the poet's tragic light resented,
The spirit that is Woman caressed his soul.

I Had a Future

O I had a future,
A future.

Gods of the imagination bring back to life
The personality of those streets,
Not any streets
But the streets of nineteen-forty.

Give the quarter-seeing eyes I looked out of,
The animal-remembering mind,
The fog through which I walked towards the mirage
That was my future.

The women I was to meet,
They were nowhere within sight.

And then the pathos of the blind soul,
Who without knowing stands in its own kingdom.

Bring me a small detail
How I felt about money,
Not frantic as later,
There was the future.

Show me the stretcher-bed I slept on
In a room on Drumcondra Road.
Let John Betjeman call for me in a car.

It is summer and the eerie beat
Of madness in Europe trembles the
Wings of the butterflies along the canal.

O I had a future.

Wet Evening in April

The birds sang in the wet trees
And as I listened to them it was a hundred years from now
And I was dead and someone else was listening to them.
But I was glad I had recorded for him the melancholy.

The Ghost Land

Not a stir, not a stir in the land,
The cloudless sky
Of a ghost world –
Businessmen hurrying to their offices,
Businessmen hurrying to their homes,

Businessmen hurrying to their golf clubs,
Their souls locked in their cars.

Not a kick, not a kick in the heart
Of the land,
But only a slow desperation –
Girls hurrying to their sodality meetings,
Girls hurrying to the theatre,
Girls with girls
Walking to their chastity graves.

Not a kick, not a stir
In heart or in air.

The Road to Hate

He said: The road you are going will lead you to Hate,
For I went down that way yesterday and saw it away
In the hollow a mile distant and I turned back
Glad of my escape.
       But I said: I will persist,
For I know a man who went down the hill into the hollow
And entered the very city of Hate
And God visited him every day out of pity
Till in the end he became a most noble saint.

The God of Poetry

I met a man upon the road
And a solemn man was he,
I said to him: you surely are
The god of poetry.

He never answered my remark,
But solemnly walked on,
Uttering words like 'splendour' and
'Picasso-fingered dawn'.

Then I walked on until I met
Another man and he
Danced with delight – this surely is
The god of poetry.

All day I walked, all day I searched,
And had no eyes to see
The genuine god who never looks
A bit like poetry.

A Ballad

O cruel are the women of Dublin's fair city,
They smile out of cars and are gone in a flash,
You know they are charming and gay in their hearts
And would laugh as vivaciously buried in chaff
As they would underneath a pink shower of confetti.

I know one in Baggot Street, a medical student
Unless I am greatly mistaken is she;
Her smile plays a tune on my trembling psyche
At thirty yards range, but she passes by me
In a frost that would make Casanova be prudent.

It's the same everywhere – the wish without will,
And it tortures, yet I would not change it for all
The women from Bond Street right down to The Mall,
For wealth is potential, not the readies at call,
I say as I walk down from Baggot Street Bridge.

Having Confessed

Having confessed, he feels
That he should go down on his knees and pray
For forgiveness for his pride, for having
Dared to view his soul from the outside.
Lie at the heart of the emotion, time

Has its own work to do. We must not anticipate
Or awaken for a moment. God cannot catch us
Unless we stay in the unconscious room
Of our hearts. We must be nothing,
Nothing that God may make us something.
We must not touch the immortal material,
We must not daydream tomorrow's judgement –
God must be allowed to surprise us.
We have sinned, sinned like Lucifer
By this anticipation. Let us lie down again
Deep in anonymous humility and God
May find us worthy material for His hand.

If Ever You Go to Dublin Town

If ever you go to Dublin town
In a hundred years or so,
Inquire for me in Baggot Street
And what I was like to know.
O he was a queer one
Fol dol the di do,
He was a queer one
I tell you.

My great-grandmother knew him well,
He asked her to come and call
On him in his flat and she giggled at the thought
Of a young girl's lovely fall.
O he was dangerous

Fol dol the di do,
He was dangerous
I tell you.

On Pembroke Road look out for my ghost
Dishevelled with shoes untied,
Playing through the railings with little children
Whose children have long since died.
O he was a nice man
Fol dol the di do,
He was a nice man
I tell you.

Go into a pub and listen well
If my voice still echoes there,
Ask the men what their grandsires thought
And tell them to answer fair.
O he was eccentric
Fol dol the di do,
He was eccentric
I tell you.

He had the knack of making men feel
As small as they really were
Which meant as great as God had made them
But as males they disliked his air.
O he was a proud one
Fol dol the di do,
He was a proud one
I tell you.

If ever you go to Dublin town
In a hundred years or so,
Sniff for my personality,
Is it vanity's vapour now?

O he was a vain one
Fol dol the di do,
He was a vain one
I tell you.

I saw his name with a hundred others
In a book in the library;
It said he had never fully achieved
His potentiality.
O he was slothful
Fol dol the di do,
He was slothful
I tell you.

He knew that posterity has no use
For anything but the soul,
The lines that speak the passionate heart,
The spirit that lives alone.
O he was a lone one
Fol dol the di do,
Yet he lived happily
I tell you.

The Rowley Mile

As I was walking down a street
Upon a summer's day
A typical girl I chanced to meet
And gathered courage to say:

'I've seen you many, many times
Upon this Rowley Mile
And I'm foolish enough to believe you love
Me for you always smile.'

Well, she gathered herself into a ball
Receding all the time.
She said: 'I beg your pardon,
I do not know what you mean.'
I stammered vainly for the right word,
I said: 'I mean to say
I'm not trying to get off with you
Or anything in that way.'

The street was full of eyes that stared
At something very odd.
I tried to imagine how little means
Such a contretemps to God.
I followed her a few slow yards,
'Please just one moment stop',
And then I dashed with urgent tread
Into a corner shop.

As I walked down that sunny street
I was a broken man
Thanks to an Irish girl
Who smiles but is true to the plan
Taught her by Old Gummy Granny –
You must try out your power with a smile,
But come to the test hard reality must
Make the pace on the Rowley Mile.

Cyrano de Bergerac

She kicked a pebble with her toe,
She tapped a railing idly –
And when we met she swerved and took
The corner very widely.
I thought that could be love; I know
The power of the male,
But without an introduction
The thing, she knows, will fail.

And so I planned for many a day
A ruse to soothe convention:
Stare up at numbers over doors
And some vague doctor mention;
Or get myself invited to
Some party where she'd be –
But all these things went down the drain
Of anti-dignity.

And then one day we actually
Did meet by introduction
And I told her with a laugh or two
She had been my distraction.
She told me I was subtle, her
Love distress to note;
She *was* in love and worried
About someone who was not.

And she always thought when looking at
My loving priestly face
That I was one who surely

Could give her love-advice . . .
And from the mirror, going out,
The lecher looked at me
And grinned before resuming
His priestly dignity.

The Hero

He was an ordinary man, a man full of humour,
Born for no high sacrifice, to be no marble god;
But all the gods had failed that harvest and someone spread the
     rumour
That he might be deluded into taking on the job.
And they came to him in the spring
And said: you are our poet-king.

Their evil weakness smiled on him and he had no answer to it,
They drove him out of corners into the public gaze;
And the more he tried to defend himself the more they cried,
     O poet,
Why must you always insult us when we only want to praise?
And he said: I wish you would
Pick on someone else to be your god.

They laughed when he told them he had no intention of dying
For virtue or truth; that his ideal would be
As a medieval Sultan, in a middle-class setting, enjoying
Many female slaves – where Luxury,
All joyful mysteries,
Takes Wisdom on her knees.

Thinking of the mean reality of middle-class life
They saw the normal as outlandish joy
And all of them embittered with a second-hand wife,
Growing literary, begged him to die
Before his vision became
The slightest bit tame.

He advised them that gods are invisibly cloaked by a crowd,
Mortality touches the conspicuous;
They had the wrong idea of a god
Who once all known becomes ridiculous.
– I am as obvious as an auctioneer
Dreaming of twenty thousand pounds a year.

At this they roared in the streets and became quite hysterical
And he knew he was the cause of this noise –
Yet he had acted reasonably, had performed no miracle,
Had spoken in a conventional voice.
And he said: surely you can
See that I am an ordinary man?

But instead they rushed off and published in all the papers
And magazines the photograph of their poet genius, god;
And all the cafés buzzed with his outrageous sayings –
He feared he was beaten and might have to take the job
For one day in the insincere city
He had an attack of self-pity.

He looked in the shoe-shop windows where all the shoes were toys,
Everything else similarly scaled down;
The hotels were doll's houses of doll's vice –
He was trapped in a pygmy town.
Vainly on all fours
He tried the small doors.

Crowds of little men went in with smooth authority
To settle this and that at boardroom tables;
Sometimes they looked up and imagined him Morality,
The silenced bishop of some heathen fables,
The ruler of the See
Of monstrous Anarchy.

Yet he found out at last the nature and the cause
Of what was and is and he no more wanted
To avoid the ludicrous cheer, the sick applause –
The sword of satire in his hand became blunted,
And for the insincere city
He felt a profound pity.

Intimate Parnassus

Men are what they are, and what they do
Is their own business. If they praise
The gods or jeer at them, the gods cannot
Be moved, involved or hurt. Serenely
The citizens of Parnassus look on,
As Homer tells us, and never laugh
When any mortal has joined the party.
What happens in the small towns –
Hate, love, envy – is not
The concern of the gods. The poet poor,
Or pushed around, or to be hanged, retains
His full reality; and his authority
Is bogus if the sonorous beat is broken

By disturbances in human hearts – his own
Is detached, experimental, subject matter
For ironic analysis, even for pity
As for some stranger's private problem.
It is not cold on the mountain, human women
Fall like ripe fruit while mere men
Are climbing out on dangerous branches
Of banking, insurance and shops; going
To the theatre; becoming
Acquainted with actors; unhappily
Pretending to a knowledge of art.
Poet, you have reason to be sympathetic –
Count them the beautiful unbroken
And then forget them
As things aside from the main purpose
Which is to be
Passive, observing with a steady eye.

On Reading a Book on Common Wild Flowers

O the prickly sow thistle that grew in the hollow of the Near Field.
I used it as a high jump coming home in the evening –
A hurdle race over the puce blossoms of the sow thistles.
Am I late?
Am I tired?
Is my heart sealed
From the ravening passion that will eat it out
Till there is not one pure moment left?

O the greater fleabane that grew at the back of the potato-pit.
I often trampled through it looking for rabbit burrows!
The burnet saxifrage was there in profusion
And the autumn gentian –
I knew them all by eyesight long before I knew their names.
We were in love before we were introduced.

Let me not moralize or have remorse, for these names
Purify a corner of my mind;
I jump over them and rub them with my hands,
And a free moment appears brand new and spacious
Where I may live beyond the reach of desire.

Narcissus and the Women

Many women circled the prison of Reflection
Where he lay among the flashing mirrors
Hoping somewhere to find some door of Action
By which he might be rescued from his errors.

Irish Stew

Our ancient civilization – and –
This Christian State of Ireland!

He said to open his oration
With protective incantation.

Then, all in the Name of God,
He turned on me a beaming broad

Face that twitched with a restive hate,
And this is what that man did state:

You're far too great a genius to
Talk of steak and onions or a stew,

Luxury would ruin your sublime
Imagination in no time.

And domesticity, wife, house, car,
We want you always as you are.

Such things don't fit into the scheme
Of one who dreams the poet's dream.

Your wildness is your great attraction,
You could not be a man of action.

Now, you'll never have to worry how to live –
A man who has so much to give.

My cousin dabbles in verse, but he
Has not your spark of poetry;

Unlike you he has not nobly strained –
But in economics he is trained;

He has a politician's mind
To deal with an ugly world designed;

Knows how to handle you great men,
Artists and masters of the pen,

Can run an office, plan a series
Of lectures for the Cork O'Learys

Or Jesuits of Clongowes College
Because he's got the practical knowledge;

And that is why he has been sent
To travel on the Continent,

To bring back the secret of great arts
To Kerry and remoter parts,

To spread in Naas and Clonakilty
News of Gigli and R. M. Rilke.

Our last art emissary whored
And that's one reason we can't afford

To risk an important man like you
In the dangerous European stew.

The Christmas Mummers

Apology for The Christmas Mummers

This is the stuff of which I was made,
The crude loud homespun bagging at the knees,
The primitive but not simple barbarities,
The casual labourer with an unskilful spade.
Unsimple ignorance was our only trade;
Our minds untrained to tensions would not seize
The string and stretch it till sincerity's
Tune to the pain-nobled end was played.
We shouted on mountains, but no god gathered
The wise sayings and the extraordinarily pure notes;
All went for nothing, a whole nation blathered
Without art, which is Character's city name.
And that is the story, the reason for the trailing coats;
The unmannerly bravado is the bluff of shame.

The Christmas Mummers

The Roomer
Room, room, my gallant boys and give us room to rhyme,
We'll show you some activity coming on this Christmastime;
We act the rich, we act the poor, the simple and the critical,
We act the scenes that lie behind the public and political,
We bring you noble statesmen and poets loused with song
And actors who make stacks of money making fun,
And if you don't believe me and give in to what I say
I'll call in Seamus O'Donovan and he'll soon clear the way.

Seamus O'Donovan

Here comes I Seamus O'Donovan – against the British menace
I fought when I was younger in the War of Independence;
Encouraged the national language, too old myself to learn it –
And if I got a pension who says I didn't earn it?
In days when 'The Emergency' was no poor cow in labour,
But war most awful threatening the world and our neighbour,
I took my musket down and joined young men who were no
    moochers
But soldiering nobly for the land into congenial futures;
My face as you can see is clear-marked old IRA,
An Irish face, good-natured, Catholic, liberal and gay;
My hair is turning whitish (though in youth severely mauled,
Oddly, no man who ever fought for Ireland goes quite bald).
For the good name of my country I am most insanely zealous
And of comrades who got richer I am not the least bit jealous,
And if you don't believe me and give in to what I say
I'll call in a Successful Statesman and he'll soon clear the way.

Successful Statesman

Here comes I a successful Statesman, from the people I am
    sprung,
My father a National Teacher learned in Gaelic rune and song;
My mother was of ancient stock and early taught to me
The fear of God and daily toil and common poverty.
By the worthy Christian Brothers my character was shaped
And we prayed for Mother Erin when by Saxons she was raped;
I played my part in the struggle – played football for my county
And won an All-Ireland medal when I was barely twenty.
And I never deserted poetry – God be good to poor Owen Roe!
And the thousand Kerry poets who were slaughtered by the foe.
And if you don't believe me and give in to what I say
I'll call in Seán Óg Ó'Gúm and he'll soon clear the way.

Seán Óg Ó'Gúm

Here comes I Seán Óg Ó'Gúm, seven pounds a week have I
Retainer from the Government for writing poetry:
I write about the tinker tribes and porter-drinking men
Who shoulder-shove their minds into the handle of my pen.
The clans are scything song again on rebel-ripened hills
And reason screams for mercy at the scratching of our quills.
We know a hundred thousand ways for saying 'Drink your liquor';
When we toss the coin of language ne'er a ha'penny comes a sticker,
And in no tin-can-dazzled dawn our holy faith is put in pawn.
No truck have we with pagans or the foreign backside-licker.
I set my boat's proud prow to sea and hoist my ballad sails
And chant on decks of destiny for the all-too-silent Gaels,
And if you don't believe me and give in to what I say
I'll call in a Famous Actor and he'll soon clear the way.

Famous Actor

Here comes I, a Famous Actor of films, stage and radio,
I was born the son of a peasant in the county of Mayo;
I am the man they call on to speak the verse of Seán
And other Gaelic poets, and lately I have done
A lot of work in English that's well out of the groove –
The popular taste in culture we are aiming to improve;
And last week when adjudicating at a Drama Festival,
I found that Irish audiences liked Eliot best of all.
I've escaped the grind of daily toil and cabins dirty, smelly,
And I'm married to a daughter of Senator O'Kelly,
And if you don't believe me and give in to what I say
I'll call in Senator O'Kelly and he'll soon clear the way.

Senator O'Kelly

Here comes I Senator O'Kelly, a simple businessman,
I make no claims to culture though I do the best I can
To foster our great artists and, though business presses so,
I go to exhibitions and I spend a lot of dough.

And one thing most I do regret, a thing to me most shocking,
And that is certain critics who are far too fond of knocking
The men who make their country known throughout the artistic
    sphere
Earning dollars with the pictures at which these fellows sneer.
As a common or garden businessman this attitude I deplore,
But I thank God for our vigilant Press which shuts on them its
    door.
And if you don't believe me and give in to what I say
I'll call in a Leading Editor and he'll soon clear the way.

Leading Editor
Here comes I a Leading Editor who knows the Irish dream,
I'm open to every idea that fits in with the regime:
The Liberal Opposition who complain of bishops' mitres
And the rising cost of turnips and the censorship on writers.
The Press is free, the radio gives them a free debate,
New Statesmanism is essential to every well-run state.
These are not Lilliputian cranks as destructive critics scream
They are the Official Liberal Opposition and part of the regime.
And if you don't believe me and give in to what I say,
Go to the bogs or Birmingham or Mountjoy right away.

Prelude

Give us another poem, he said,
Or they will think your muse is dead;
Another middle-age departure
Of Apollo from the trade of archer.

Bring out a book as soon as you can
To let them see you're a living man,
Whose comic spirit is untamed
Though sadness for a little claimed
The precedence; and tentative
You pulled your punch and wondered if
Old cunning Silence might not be
A better bet than poetry.

You have not got the countenance
To hold the angle of pretence,
That angry bitter look for one
Who knows that art's a kind of fun;
That all true poems laugh inwardly
Out of grief-born intensity.
Dullness alone can get you beat
And so can humour's counterfeit.
You have not got a chance with fraud
And might as well be true to God.

Then link your laughter out of doors
In sunlight past the sick-faced whores
Who chant the praise of love that isn't
And bring their bastards to be Christened
At phoney founts by bogus priests
With rites mugged up by journalists.
Walk past professors looking serious
Fondling an unpublished thesis –
'A child! my child! my darling son'
Some Poets of Nineteen Hundred and One.

Note well the face profoundly grave,
An empty mind can house a knave.

Be careful to show no defiance,
They've made pretence into a science:
Card-sharpers of the art committees
Working all the provincial cities,
They cry 'Eccentric' if they hear
A voice that seems at all sincere,
Fold up their table and their gear
And with the money disappear.

But satire is unfruitful prayer,
Only wild shoots of pity there,
And you must go inland and be
Lost in compassion's ecstasy,
Where suffering soars in summer air –
The millstone has become a star.

Count then your blessings, hold in mind
All that has loved you or been kind:
Those women on their mercy missions,
Rescue work with kiss or kitchens,
Perceiving through the comic veil
The poet's spirit in travail.

Gather the bits of road that were
Not gravel to the traveller
But eternal lanes of joy
On which no man who walks can die.
Bring in the particular trees
That caught you in their mysteries,
And love again the weeds that grew
Somewhere specially for you.
Collect the river and the stream
That flashed upon a pensive theme,
And a positive world make,
A world man's world cannot shake,

And do not lose love's resolution
Though face to face with destitution.

If Platitude should claim a place
Do not denounce his humble face;
His sentiments are well-intentioned,
He has a part in the larger legend.

So now my gentle tiger burning
In the forest of no-yearning,
Walk on serenely, do not mind
That Promised Land you thought to find,
Where the worldly-wise and rich take over
The mundane problems of the lover.
Ignore Power's schismatic sect
Lovers alone lovers protect.

One Wet Summer

Another summer, another July,
People going on holiday, women in light dresses.
How I once jealously feared for them moving under the printed
     cotton,
Limp, unresisting to any man's caresses.

I would have one of my own,
And then like other men I could make cynical remarks
At the dangers they ran and never be worried about summer
And what happens in the shelter of parks.

As it is I praise the rain
For washing out the bank holiday with its moral risks.
It is not a nice attitude but it is conditioned by circumstances
And by a childhood perverted by Christian moralists.

After Forty Years of Age

There was a time when a mood recaptured was enough,
Just to be able to hold momentarily November in the woods
Or a street we once made our own through being in love.

But that is not enough now. The job is to answer questions.
Experience. Tell us what life has taught you. Not just about
    persons –
Which is futile anyway in the long run – but a concrete, as it were,
    essence.

The role is that of prophet and saviour. To smelt in passion
The commonplaces of life. To take over the functions of a god in a
    new fashion.
Ah! there is the question to speculate upon in lieu of an answer.

An Insult

I came to a great house on the edge of a park,
Thinking on Yeats's dream great house where all
Nobility was protected by ritual,
Though all lay drunk on the floor and in the dark
Tough louts and menial minds in the shrubberies lurk
And negative eunuchs hate in an outer hall.
The poet and lover is safe though from grace he fall
Temporarily. The Evil Barbarian dare not work
The servile spell, the insult of a fool,
To which there is no answer but to pray
For guidance through the parks of everyday,
To be silent till the soul itself forgives,
To learn again there is no golden rule
For keeping out of suffering – if one lives.

Nineteen Fifty-Four

Nineteen Fifty-Four hold on till I try
To formulate some theory about you. A personal matter:
My lamp of contemplation you sought to shatter,
To leave me groping in madness under a low sky.
O I wish I could laugh! O I wish I could cry!
Or find some formula, some mystical patter
That would organize a perspective from this hellish scatter –
Everywhere I look a part of me is exiled from the I.

Therefore I must tell you before you depart my position;
Making the statement is enough – there are no answers
To any real question. But tonight I cannot sleep;
Two hours ago I heard the late homing dancers.
O Nineteen Fifty-Four you leave and will not listen,
And do not care whether I curse or weep.

House Party to Celebrate the Destruction of the Roman Catholic Church in Ireland

Her book was out, and did she devastate
The Roman Catholic Church on every page!
And in Seamus's house they met to celebrate
With giggles high the dying monster's rage.

When Seamus gazed upon this woman he
Reflected on one absolute disgrace
Outside the bounds of every decency –
'A female replica of Cromwell's face'

Was how some rural savage had described
This noble woman – she was not blotched,
Her wart was a beauty mole. He had been bribed
To rhyme his sneer. Some Bishop had been touched.

So terrible was Seamus's emotion,
The sherry glass was dancing in his hand –
The Jansenistic priesthood of the nation
Had perished by this woman writer's hand.

With fighting admiration in his eyes
He could not see his wife but only Her.
He stammered: 'You did more than satirise.
Great artist! The Irish Voltaire.'

The reviews were coming in by every post,
Warm and fulsome – Seamus read extracts:
'The Roman Catholic Hierarchy must
Be purple now with rage. She states the facts

With wit, and wit is what they cannot bear'.
In far off parishes of Cork and Kerry
Old priests walked homeless in the winter air
As Seamus poured another pale dry sherry.

1956—9

The Hospital

A year ago I fell in love with the functional ward
Of a chest hospital: square cubicles in a row,
Plain concrete, wash basins – an art lover's woe,
Not counting how the fellow in the next bed snored.
But nothing whatever is by love debarred,
The common and banal her heat can know.
The corridor led to a stairway and below
Was the inexhaustible adventure of a gravelled yard.

This is what love does to things: the Rialto Bridge,
The main gate that was bent by a heavy lorry,
The seat at the back of a shed that was a suntrap.
Naming these things is the love-act and its pledge;
For we must record love's mystery without claptrap,
Snatch out of time the passionate transitory.

Leaves of Grass

When I was growing up and for many years after
I was led to believe that poems were thin,
Dreary, irrelevant, well out of the draught of laughter,
With headquarters the size of the head of a pin.
I do not wonder now that my mother moaned
To see her beloved son an idiot boy;
He could not see what was before his eyes, the ground

Tumultuous with living, infinite as Cleopatra's variety.
He hit upon the secret door that leads to the heaven
Of human satisfaction, a purpose, and did not know it;
An army of grass blades were at his call, million on million
Kept saying to him, we nearly made Whitman a poet.
Years after in Dublin in summer past midnight o'clock
They called to him vainly from kerbstones on Bachelor's Walk.

October

O leafy yellowness you create for me
A world that was and now is poised above time,
I do not need to puzzle out Eternity
As I walk this arboreal street on the edge of a town.
The breeze, too, even the temperature
And pattern of movement, is precisely the same
As broke my heart for youth passing. Now I am sure
Of something. Something will be mine wherever I am.
I want to throw myself on the public street without caring
For anything but the prayering that the earth offers.
It is October over all my life and the light is staring
As it caught me once in a plantation by the fox coverts.
A man is ploughing ground for winter wheat
And my nineteen years weigh heavily on my feet.

Birth

We will not hold an inquest on the past –
The Word died, the mistake was made, the sin
Was committed as the wheel turned again
And again, exactly as it had turned last.
In the mornings we made promises to ourselves as the fresh
Air of the street gave us that springtime feeling,
That is to say, sad hope. Our wills were willing
And plenty of years in the future said, wish your wish.
Yet there was something of the dead past polluting
The New Word we had created out of water and the spirit
And everything seemed over bar the shouting,
When out of the holy mouth came angelic grace
And the will that had fought had found new merit
And all sorts of beautiful things appeared in that place.

Requiem for a Mill

They took away the water-wheel,
Scrap-ironed all the corn-mill;
The water now cascades with no
Audience pacing to and fro
Taking in with casual glance
Experience.

The cold wet blustery winter day
And all that's happening will stay
Alive in the mind: the bleak
Water-flushed meadows speak
An enduring story
To a man indifferent in a doorway.

Packaged, pre-cooked flakes have left
A land of that old mill bereft.
The ghosts that were so local coloured
Hiding behind bags of pollard
Have gone from those empty walls.
The weir still curves its waterfalls
But lets them drop in the tailrace
No longer wildly chivalrous.

And with this mention we withdraw
To things above the temporal law.

Question to Life

Surely you would not ask me to have known
Only the passion of primrose banks in May
Which are merely a point of departure for the play
And yearning poignancy when on their own.
Yet when all is said and done a considerable
Portion of living is found in inanimate
Nature, and a man need not feel miserable
If fate should have decided on this plan of it.

Then there is always the passing gift of affection
Tossed from the windows of high charity
In the office girl and civil servant section
And these are no despisable commodity.
So be reposed and praise, praise, praise
The way it happened and the way it is.

Come Dance with Kitty Stobling

No, no, no, I know I was not important as I moved
Through the colourful country, I was but a single
Item in the picture, the namer not the beloved.
O tedious man with whom no gods commingle.
Beauty, who has described beauty? Once upon a time
I had a myth that was a lie but it served:
Trees walking across the crests of hills and my rhyme
Cavorting on mile-high stilts and the unnerved
Crowds looking up with terror in their rational faces.
O dance with Kitty Stobling, I outrageously
Cried out-of-sense to them, while their timorous paces
Stumbled behind Jove's page boy paging me.
I had a very pleasant journey, thank you sincerely
For giving me my madness back, or nearly.

Is

The important thing is not
To imagine one ought
Have something to say,
A raison d'être, a plot for the play.
The only true teaching
Subsists in watching
Things moving or just colour
Without comment from the scholar.
To look on is enough
In the business of love.
Casually remark
On a deer running in a park;
Mention water again
Always virginal,
Always original,
It washes out Original Sin.
Name for the future
The everydays of nature
And without being analytic
Create a great epic.
Girls in red blouses,
Steps up to houses,
Sunlight round gables,
Gossip's young fables,
The life of a street.

O wealthy me! O happy state!
With an inexhaustible theme
I'll die in harness,
I'll die in harness with my scheme.

To Hell with Commonsense

More kicks than pence
We get from commonsense;
Above its door is writ
All hope abandon. It
Is a bank will refuse a post
Dated cheque of the Holy Ghost.
Therefore I say to hell
With all reasonable
Poems in particular;
We want no secular
Wisdom plodded together
By concerned fools. Gather
No moss you rolling stones.
Nothing thought out atones
For no flight
In the light.
Let them wear out nerve and bone
Those who would have it that way
But in the end nothing that they
Have achieved will be in the shake up,
In the final Wake Up.
And I have a feeling
That through the hole in reason's ceiling
We can fly to knowledge
Without ever going to college.

Canal Bank Walk

Leafy-with-love banks and the green waters of the canal
Pouring redemption for me, that I do
The will of God, wallow in the habitual, the banal,
Grow with nature again as before I grew.
The bright stick trapped, the breeze adding a third
Party to the couple kissing on an old seat,
And a bird gathering materials for the nest for the Word,
Eloquently new and abandoned to its delirious beat.
O unworn world enrapture me, encapture me in a web
Of fabulous grass and eternal voices by a beech,
Feed the gaping need of my senses, give me ad lib
To pray unselfconsciously with overflowing speech,
For this soul needs to be honoured with a new dress woven
From green and blue things and arguments that cannot be proven.

Dear Folks

Just a line to remind my friends that after much trouble
Of one kind and another I am back in circulation.
I have recovered most of my heirlooms from the heaps of rubble
That once was the house where I lived in the name of a nation.
And precious little I assure you was worth mind storage:
The images of half a dozen women who fell for the unusual,
For the Is that Is and the laughter-smothered courage,
The poet's. And I also found some crucial

Documents of sad evil that may yet
For all their ugliness and vacuous leers
Fuel the fires of comedy. The main thing is to continue,
To walk Parnassus right into the sunset
Detached in love where pygmies cannot pin you
To the ground like Gulliver. So good luck and cheers.

Song at Fifty

It came as a pleasant surprise
To find experience
Where I had feared that I
Had no such currency,
Had idled to a void
Without a wife or child.
I had been looking at
Fields, gates, lakes, all that
Was part and parcel of
The wild breast of love.
In other fellows' wives
I lived a many lives,
And here another cries:
My husband I despise
And truth is my true
Husband is you.

So I take my cloak of gold
And stride across the world,
A knight of chivalry
Seeking some devilry;

The winter trees rise up
And wave me on, a clap
Of falling rock declares
Enthusiasm; flares
Announce a reception committee
For me entering a city.
And all this for an unthrifty
Man turned of fifty;
An undisciplined person
Through futile excitements arsing
Finds in his spendthrift purse
A bankbook writ in verse
And borrowers of purity
Offering substantial security
To him who just strayed
Through a lifetime without a trade,
Him, him the ne'er-
Do-well a millionaire.

Freedom

Take me to the top of the high hill,
Mount Olympus, laughter-roaring, unsolemn,
Where no one is angry and satirical
About a mortal creature on a tall column.

Lines Written on a Seat on the Grand Canal, Dublin

'Erected to the Memory of Mrs Dermod O'Brien'

O commemorate me where there is water,
Canal water preferably, so stilly
Greeny at the heart of summer. Brother
Commemorate me thus beautifully
Where by a lock Niagarously roars
The falls for those who sit in the tremendous silence
Of mid-July. No one will speak in prose
Who finds his way to these Parnassian islands.
A swan goes by head low with many apologies,
Fantastic light looks through the eyes of bridges –
And look! a barge comes bringing from Athy
And other far-flung towns mythologies.
O commemorate me with no hero-courageous
Tomb – just a canal-bank seat for the passer-by.

The Self-slaved

Me I will throw away.
Me sufficient for the day,
The sticky self that clings,
Adhesions on the wings.
To love and adventure,

To go on the grand tour,
A man must be free
From self-necessity.

See over there
A created splendour
Made by one individual
From things residual
With all the various
Qualities hilarious
Of what
Hitherto was not:

A November mood
As by one man understood;
Familiar, an old custom,
Leaves falling, a white frosting
Bringing a sanguine dream,
A new beginning with an old theme.

Throw away thy sloth
Self, carry off my wrath
With its self-righteous
Satirizing blotches.
No self, no self-exposure,
The weakness of the proser,
But undefeatable
By means of the beatable.

I will have love, have love
From anything made of,
And a life with a shapely form
With gaiety and charm
And capable of receiving
With grace the grace of living,

And wild moments too
Self when freed from you.
Prometheus calls me on.
Prometheus calls me: Son,
We'll both go off together
In this delightful weather.

The One

Green, blue, yellow and red –
God is down in the swamps and marshes,
Sensational as April and almost incred-
    ible the flowering of our catharsis.
A humble scene in a backward place
Where no one important ever looked;
The raving flowers looked up in the face
Of the One and the Endless, the Mind that has baulked
The profoundest of mortals. A primrose, a violet,
A violent wild iris – but mostly anonymous performers,
Yet an important occasion as the Muse at her toilet
Prepared to inform the local farmers
That beautiful, beautiful, beautiful God
Was breathing His love by a cut-away bog.

Yellow Vestment

Lately I have been travelling by a created guidance,
I invented a Superintendent, symbol henceforth vaster
Than Jupiter, Prometheus or a Chinese deity in alabaster.
For love's sake we must only consider whatever widens
The field of the faithful's activity. See over there
Water-lilies waiting to be enchanted by a folk song chanted.
On the road we walk nobody is unwanted;
With no hate in his heart or resentment each may wear
The arrogant air that goes with a yellow vestment.
Do not be worried about what the neighbours will say,
Deliver your judgment, you are independent
Of the man in the pub whose word is essential to happiness,
Who gives you existence. O sing to me some roundelay
And wear with grace the power-invoking habit.

Love in a Meadow

She waved her body in the circle sign
Of love purely born without side;
The earth's contour she orbited to my pride,
Sin and unsin.
But the critic asking questions ran
From the fright of the dawn
To weep later on an urban lawn
For the undone

God-gifted man.
O the river flowed round and round
The low meadows filled with buttercups
In a place called Toprass.
I was born on high ground.

Miss Universe

I learned, I learned – when one might be inclined
To think, too late, you cannot recover your losses –
I learned something of the nature of God's mind,
Not the abstract Creator but He who caresses
The daily and nightly earth; He who refuses
To take failure for an answer till again and again is worn.
Love is waiting for you, waiting for the violence that she chooses
From the tepidity of the common round beyond exhaustion or
    scorn.
What was once is still and there is no need for remorse;
There are no recriminations in Heaven. O the sensual throb
Of the explosive body, the tumultuous thighs!
Adown a summer lane comes Miss Universe,
She whom no lecher's art can rob
Though she is not the virgin who was wise.

Winter

Christmas, someone mentioned, is almost upon us
And looking out my window I saw that Winter had landed
Complete with the grey cloak and the bare tree sonnet,
A scroll of bark hanging down to the knees as he scanned it.
The gravel in the yard was pensive, annoyed to be crunched
As people with problems in their faces drove by in cars,
Yet I with such solemnity around me refused to be bunched,
In fact was inclined to give the go-by to bars.
Yes, there were things in that winter arrival that made me
Feel younger, less of a failure, it was actually earlier
Than many people thought; there were possibilities
For love, for South African adventure, for fathering a baby,
For taking oneself in hand, catching on without a scare me, or
Taking part in a world war, joining up at the start of hostilities.

Living in the Country

Opening

It was the Warm Summer, that landmark
In a child's mind, an infinite day,
Sunlight and burnt grass,
Green grasshoppers on the railway slopes,
The humming of wild bees,
The whole summer during the school holidays

Till the blackberries appeared.
Yes, a tremendous time that summer stands
Beyond the grey finities of normal weather.

The Main Body

It's not nearly as bad as you'd imagine
Living among small farmers in the north of Ireland.
They are for the most part the ordinary frightened,
Blind brightened, referred to sometimes socially
As the underprivileged.
They cannot perceive Irony or even Satire;
They start up with insane faces if
You break the newspaper moral code.
'Language', they screech, 'you effing so and so',
And you withdraw into a precarious silence,
Organizing in your mind quickly, for the situation is tense,
The theological tenets of the press.

There's little you can do about some
Who roar horribly as you enter a bar
Incantations of ugliness, words of half a syllable,
Locked in malicious muteness full of glare.
And your dignity thinks of giving up the beer.
But I, trained in the slum pubs of Dublin
Among the most offensive class of all –
The artisans – am equal to this problem;
I let it ride and there is nothing over.
I understand through all these years
That my difference in their company is an intrusion
That tears at the sentimental clichés;
They can see my heart squirm when their star rendites
The topmost twenty in the lowered lights.
No, sir, I did not come unprepared.

Oddly enough I begin to think of Saint Francis
Moving in this milieu (of his own time of course).
How did he work the oracle?
Was he an old fraud, a non-poet
Who is loved for his non-ness
Like any performer?

I protest here and now and for ever
On behalf of all my peoples who believe in Verse
That my intention is not satire but humaneness,
An eagerness to understand more about sad man,
Frightened man, the workers of the world,
Without being savaged in the process.
Broadness is my aim, a broad road where the many
Can see life easier – generally.

Here I come to a sticky patch,
A personal matter that perhaps
Might be left as an unrevealed hinterland,
For our own misfortunes are mostly unimportant.
But that wouldn't do.
So with as little embarrassment as possible I tell
How I was done out of a girl,
Not as before by a professional priest but by
The frightened artisan's morality.

It was this way.
She, a shopgirl of nineteen or less,
Became infatuated by the old soldier,
The wide travelled, the sin-wise.
Desdemona-Othello idea.
O holy spirit of infatuation
God's gift to his poetic nation!

One day her boss caught her glance.
'You're looking in his eyes', he said.
From then on all the powers of the lower orders –
Perhaps all orders – were used to deprive me of my prize,
Agamemnon's Briseis.
It soured me a bit as I had
Everything planned, no need to mention what,
Except that it was August evening under whitethorn
And early blackberries.

In many ways it is a good thing to be cast into exile
Among strangers
Who have no inkling
Of The Other Man concealed
Monstrously musing in a field.
For me they say a Rosary
With many a glossary.

Lecture Hall

To speak in summer in a lecture hall
About literature and its use
I pick my brains and tease out all
To see if I can choose
Something untarnished, some new news

From experience that has been immediate,
Recent, something that makes
The listener or reader

Impregnant, something that reinstates
The poet. A few words like birth-dates

That bring him back in the public mind,
I mean the mind of the dozen or so
Who constantly listen out for the two-lined
Message that announces the gusto
Of the dead arisen into the sun-glow.

Someone in America will note
The apparent miracle. In a bar
In Greenwich Village some youthful poet
Will mention it, and a similar
In London or wherever they are,

Those pickers-up of messages that produce
The idea that underneath the sun
Things can be new as July dews –
Out of the frowsy, the second-hand won . . .
Keep at it, keep at it, while the heat is on,

I say to myself as I consider
Virginal crevices in my brain
Where the never-exposed will soon be a mother.
I search for that which has no stain,
Something discovered vividly and sudden.

1960–67

News Item

In Islington for the moment I reside,
A hen's race from Cheapside
Where Tom the peeping sun first eyed.

Where Gilpin's horse had bolted
All the traffic halted;
The man on board was malted.

And in these romantic lots
I run into Paul Potts
Noticing the pull of roots.

I have taken roots of love
And will find it pain to move.
Betjeman, you've missed much of

The secrets of London while
Old churches you beguile.
I'll show you a holier aisle –

The length of Gibson Square
Caught in November's stare.
That would set you to prayer.

Dickens – all the clichés
Revert to the living species,
Ideas with the impact of Nietzsche's.

I walk in Islington Green,
Finest landscape you ever seen;
I'm as happy as I've ever been.

Mermaid Tavern

No System, no Plan,
Yeatsian invention,
No all-over
Organizational prover.
Let words laugh
And people be stimulated by our stuff.

Michelangelo's Moses
Is one of the poses
Of Hemingway
Jungle-crashing after prey.
Beckett's garbage-can
Contains all our man
Who without fright on his face
Dominates the place
And makes all feel
That all is well.

Yet without smuggery
Or the smirk of buggery
Or any other aid
We have produced our god.
And everyone present
Becomes godded and pleasant
Confident, gay –
No remorse that a day
Can show no output
Except from the gut.

In the Name of The Father,
The Son and The Mother,
We explode
Ridiculously, uncode
A habit and find therein
A successful human being.

Literary Adventures

I am here in a garage in Monaghan.
It is June and the weather is warm,
Just a little bit cloudy. There's the sun again
Lifting to importance my sixteen acre farm.
There are three swallows' nests in the rafters above me
And the first clutches are already flying.
Spread this news, tell all if you love me,
You who knew that when sick I was never dying
(Nae gane, nae gane, nae frae us torn
But taking a rest like John Jordan).
                                    Other exclusive
News stories that cannot be ignored:
I climbed Woods' Hill and the elusive
Underworld of the grasses could be heard;
John Lennon shouted across the valley.
Then I saw a New June Moon, quite as stunning
As when young we blessed the sight as something holy . . .
Sensational adventure that is only beginning.

For I am taking this evening walk through places
High up among the Six Great Wonders,
The power privileges, the unborn amazes,
The unplundered,
Where man with no meaning blooms
Large in the eyes of his females:
He doesn't project, nor even assumes
The loss of one necessary believer.
It's as simple as that, it's a matter
Of walking with the little gods, the ignored
Who are so seldom asked to write the letter
Containing the word.
O only free gift! no need for Art any more
When Authority whispers like Tyranny at the end of a bar.

Sensational Disclosures!

(Kavanagh tells all)

Kavanagh tells all,
Lays bare his soul
For the good of his neighbours
And the Sunday papers.
Patiently he labours
To advise and warn
Poets soft in the horn.
Rising from his own dirt
He sends this sensational report:

He frittered away
A talent that could flay
D. J. Enright – say;
He could disburse
A fabulosity of verse,
Could swallow without dodgery
Ted Hughes's menagerie,
He often spat forth
Lions of more wrath.

But Kavanagh, the dog,
Took to the grog,
Leaving Larkin and Logue
Manufacturing fog,
And even MacNeice
Making ground in the race.

But he'll have the last laugh
On Davie and Hough,
For as he went wandering
In a valley, deep thundering
From long-muted fellows
Conspired in some hello's
To halt him as he rambled,
Drank brandy and gambled:

O Kavanagh repent
And start to invent
An amenable myth
Of everyday width
To meet every condition
Outside genuine passion.
Learn to shovel
A bulldozer novel.

Make critical works
Like those industrious jerks
Who don't even relax
When they go to the jakes.

Gladden our days
With musical plays –
And profoundest believer
Write prayers for the Beaver.
And then of that sum
Make a megaton bomb.

So he sailed up the Cydnus
To Chatto and Windus
And with one cannonade
Wrecked the critical trade.

Rumble and roar
In the poetry war.
American bums
Change the angle of thumbs
And get on the blower
To find out the score
(Post Spanish Civil War).
Oscar Williams is sore,
Screaming to harass
The heart of Alvarez,
Starts to eat till he'll founder
The files of *Encounter.*
'Why wasn't I told
Of new gallups polled?'

The battle is on,
There are gasps from Thom Gunn,

Elizabeth Jennings
Suspends all her pennings,
To meet new assessments
Edith burns her vestments.

And that's how it was
When Kavanagh uprose
From his dosshouse of filth
In vulgar good health.
Next week he'll reveal
All about the smell
From Soviet poets who rebel
Against what is dead,
Reminiscent of Hampstead.

Tame, tame, tame, tame,
Kavanagh lifts the lid of same,
Exposes all the guilty men,
The selectors of the team.

The Same Again

I have my friends, my public, and they are waiting
For me to come again as their one and only bard
With a new statement that will repay all the waitment
While I was hitting the bottle hard.
I know it is not right to be light and flippant;
There are people in the streets who steer by my star.
There was nothing they could do but view me while I threw

Back large whiskeys in the corner of a smoky bar.
And if only I would get drunk it wouldn't be so bad;
With a pain in my stomach I wasn't even comic,
Swallowing every digestive pill to be had.
Some of my friends stayed faithful but quite a handful
Looked upon it as the end: I could quite safely be
Dismissed a dead loss in the final up toss.
He's finished and that's definitely.

Thank You, Thank You

. . . Particularly if yourself
Have been left as they call it on the shelf,
All God's chillun got wings,
So the black Alabaman sings.

Down Grafton Street on Saturdays
Don't grieve like Marcus Aurelius
Who said that though he grew old and grey
The people on the Appian Way
Were always the same pleasant age,
Twenty-four on average.

I can never help reflecting
On coming back in another century
From now and feeling comfortable
At a buzzing coffee table,
Students in 2056
With all the old eternal tricks.

The thing that I most glory in
Is this exciting, unvarying
Quality that withal
Is completely original.

For what it teaches is just this:
We are not alone in our loneliness;
Others have been here and known
Griefs we thought our special own,
Problems that we could not solve,
Lovers that we could not have,
Pleasures that we missed by inches.
Come I'm beginning to get pretentious,
Beginning to message forth instead
Of expressing how glad
I am to have lived to feel the radiance
Of a holy hearing audience
And delivered God's commands
Into those caressing hands,
My personality that's to say
All that is mine exclusively.
What wisdom's ours if such there be
Is a flavour of personality.
I thank you and I say how proud
That I have been by fate allowed
To stand here having the joyful chance
To claim my inheritance,
For most have died the day before
The opening of that holy door.

About Reason, Maybe

The day I walked out on Reason – that old plodder –
(But you didn't)
Was the best day of my life; it would take years
To tell of the dirty he did on me, the love-fodder
That other bulls backchewed for me in several gears.
(Catholic peasant)
It is too embarrassing to talk about love misses
And pleases those we ought not entertain.
She gave herself! Oh no! There were only kisses.
The listener cannot endure the possible gain.
To tell the tale is needless repetition.
But they did come with all heroic violence
(For that I'll vouch
On any couch)
But Reason always intruded on the session,
Or perhaps it was the conscience of cold climates.
(Unwilling saint,
A moot point)
Well, call it what you like.

That Garage

The lilacs by the gate,
The summer sun again,
The swallows in and out
Of the garage where I am.
The sounds of land activity,
Machinery in gear;
This is not longevity
But infinity.
Perhaps a little bit
Too facilely romantic;
We must stop and struggle with
A mood that's going frantic,
Getting Georgian,
Richard Church and Binyon.
O stand and plan
More difficult dominion.

In Blinking Blankness: Three Efforts

I

I am here all morning with the familiar
Blank page in front of me; I have perused
An American anthology for stimulation,
But the result is not encouraging as it used

To be when Walter Lowenfels' falling down words
Like ladders excited me to chance my arm
With nouns and verbs.
But the wren, the wren got caught in the furze
And the eagle turned turkey on my farm.

II

Last summer I made a world fresh and fair,
(As the daughters of Erin) completely equipped
With everything for the full life. A wealth of experience
Of every kind waiting to be tapped.
I had a story, a career
Shaped like a statesman's for the biographer.
I had done all things in my time
And had not yet reached my prime.

III

Nature is not enough, I've used up lanes,
Waters that run in rivers or are stagnant;
But I have no message and the sins
Of no red idea can make me pregnant.
So I sit tight to manufacture
A world word-by-word-machine-to-live-in structure –
That may in any garden be assembled –
Where critics looking through the glass can lecture
On poets X, Y and Z therein entempled.

The Poet's Ready Reckoner

Nothing more to be done in that particular
Direction, nothing now but prayer –
Watching, regarding, piecing together new curricula,
An un-angry enumerator,
Handling all sorts of littleness as it has to be handled,
As if it were in the eyes
Enormous as an English biographer's tittle-tattle,
All held low so gossip can settle
Close in the nest.
I, brooding, must itemise,
Consider every colour and marking,
Search out for letters,
Pretend I am interested in important writers.
        That's not the game no more,
        We have no game no more.
Must catch that rhyme that up there I left parking.
        We have no game no more.
        Someone stole our game
        And left us high and dry
        On a beliefless shore,
        But it ain't no shame.
Plainly the only thing is not to be a bore
To ourselves; no more to it than that,
I have to live here in the country till I get a flat.

When first walking along these roads,
Nobody but myself walked there,
But wait a minute, an hour, a day,
There are men and women behaving,
There are girls in troubled love,

And all that I need to do is to weave the action
And many may do things quite valuable.
Form.
Life At Work – Do Not Disturb.
I am independent now.
I know what I must write if I can.
This is the beginning of my Five-Year Plan,
Concerned am I with the activities of my own man.

And a week ago I idled,
That is to say I roared and cursed over the position.
Broke, I had a good excuse for not caring.
Arts Council croppers harvesting and sharing
And my deserted village all ill-faring,
Activity on every front
And nought for the poor bastard who bore the brunt
Of the day's battle – blood and sweat and grunt.
Satire a desert that yields no —

As I have mentioned on many an occasion
Living in the country is a hard old station.
In the pubs everyone talks about age,
My age, they know it to a day,
No use lying on that score,
I could get away from it all if I had a motor.

I must remember to absorb
Like a sponge, not disturb
By projecting my knowledge;
It's hard work at Experience's college.

When drawn into involvement with the barmaid
By sharp-nosed fellows from the Assistant Mountains
Of Castleblayney,

I will let the embarrassment run its course,
Be rather glad,
A little of this is good.
To be always protected by a bodyguard
Of reserve, remoteness – putting them in their place
With a word from There
Is quite unhard,
But no use when you return to a vacant room.

Now that I've cottoned on to holy hoarding
Pelman himself could not increase my wording.
To take it at its least value
I never suffer now from malnu-
Trition. Or need for grog.
I make a product I can easily flog.
I am a small country exporting
The pill of meaning to those
Whom the condition is hurting.
At this moment I can make spells;
Whatever I say goes.
Come London-Irish to me, your voided souls
Shall not be left unfilled,
I am more than a pub or club,
I am the madhouse that spilled,
(Spills) the true reason,
The abandoned laughing of the free:
You were behaned in Egypt
And the alien-milled
Corn had no vitamins of hope.
You're ill poor folks and suffering from gripe.
And all this is a mere side-product. Into me never entered
Care for you. I am self-centred.

But bunch of bums
I throw you these bewitching crumbs.
I give you the womb
Of the poem.

In the disused railway siding
(O railway that came up from Enniskillen)
A new living is spreading,
Dandelions that grow from wagon-grease.
I stand on the platform
And peace, perfect peace,
Descends on me.

I said to Maggie, a most purist maid,
Can you explain the modern parade
Of tycoons sultaning it with shabby whores,
Notorious nobodys in a world of bores?
She said that that was twentieth-century play
As we lay together on an ex-railway.
She said all public heroes were the same,
From pimp descended and the poxy dame,
Glittering in dinner dress in brass tiaras,
No poet could be interested in those arses.
I saw that this was probably the case;
Private beauty and green happiness
Demand much courage. And I recalled
Being asked by poor fellows if I willed
Their right to enjoy a picture, play or book,
So glad when I gave the green light were those folk.
They had enjoyed that most uproarious play
And were so glad that they had laughed.
                                        Away!
Begone dull care thou hast not got a chance,

The rapturous eagles soar us up from Hence,
>   To Thence
>   From Sense.

My love lies at the gates of foam,
The last dear wreck of day,
And William H. Burroughs collages the poem
As the curfew tolls the knell of Gray.

A Summer Morning Walk

The sun is hot, long days, yet summer
Finds me very little dumber
Than last winter in grey old London.

Lying on a bed in a basement, unable
To lift my sickness to a fable,
Hating the sight of a breakfast table.

On Christmas Day stretched out, how awful,
Not heeding the Church's orders lawful
While everyone else is having a crawful.

It is black all round as terror-stricken
I climb stone steps, trying not to weaken,
My legs are taking a terrible licking.

To the King Edward, empty of pudds,
Two friends and I in crumpled duds
Go to talk with John Heath-Stubbs.

O Charles Dickens with your Scrooge
I would gladly have taken refuge,
I was as sick as the devil's puke.

I try to be merry those three lit hours
Then back to the subterranean fires
Drinking whisky to the sound of lyres.

Odd how such things six months later
Leap up as laughter's instigator
From the depths of that Paddington crater.

I must avoid being unfrank
The plain truth is that I drank
More than would kill a New York yank.

And verse that can redeem a soul
And make a body beautiful
I did not work at it at all.

O there is a Muse not good and gracious
But long-suffering and tenacious,
She will not have a man stay stocious.

I hope I am not being clammy,
The whisky bottle I loved like mammy,
The curse of drink! let's not get hammy.

I just want to assure all
That a poem made is a cure-all
Of any soul-sickness. Toolooral!

Today in the street I was astonished
The years had left me so unpunished,
I was in love with women – honest!

The Word is the messenger of the eye.
The old canal is as full of blue sky
As a year ago and so kind to I.

That Grand Canal into which I was pushed
At wetting me must have surely blushed.
The men who did the job were cursed:

I had praised it in many a sonnet
And the dear swans that lived upon it –
So for the grudgers to hell or Connaught!

Now I must speak to people but keep intact
The virginal knowledge, converse about fact,
Newspaper news of some international pact.

It is only twelve o'clock noon
And I have experienced about one
Millionth of a day begun.

I meet a man whom I once had pumped
With ideas, he was sad and humped
Like a market that had downward slumped.

The ideas I had upon him forced
Were gone and left him much worse, the worst,
And to think how amusingly he had discoursed.

Very nearly a poet, complete with irony,
Knowledged in every literary joinery,
He used to dress in poetic finery.

And then he leaked and, although I strove
To fill him with the breath of love,
The fatal puncture still blew off.

It was sad to see the empty bag
Blown about like a dirty rag.
But let us be humble and never brag.

The way things were going he thought my stuff
Contained far too much Parnassian guff,
As a businessman he had had enough.

So I went on my way carrying the flame
On to the ultimate Olympic Game
Where no one belonging ever gives in.

Out of weakness more than muscle,
Relentlessly men continue to tussle
With the human-eternal puzzle.

There were gulls on the pond in St Stephen's Park
And many things worth a remark.
I sat on a deck-chair and started to work

On a morning's walk not quite effectual,
A little too unselectual,
But what does it count in the great perpetual?

I must be content with the roses –
But sitting in deck-chairs, Holy Moses!
University girls here in roly-poses.

I certainly enjoyed myself thoroughly,
Rambling idly and rather amorally
For a whole hour. Now surely

I can lie on the grass, feel no remorse
For idling, I have worked at verse
And exorcised a winter's curse.

Personal Problem

To take something as a subject, indifferent
To personal affection, I have been considering
Some old saga as an instrument
To play upon without the person suffering
From the tiring years. But I can only
Tell of my problem without solving
Anything. If I could rewrite a famous tale
Or perhaps return to a midnight calving,
This cow sacred on a Hindu scale –
So there it is my friends. What am I to do
With the void growing more awful every hour?
I lacked a classical discipline. I grew
Uncultivated and now the soil turns sour,
Needs to be revived by a power not my own,
Heroes enormous who do astounding deeds –
Out of this world. Only thus can I attune
To despair an illness like winter alone in Leeds.

Yeats

Yeats, it was very easy for you to be frank,
With your sixty years and loves (like Robert Graves).
It was thin and, in fact, you have never put the tank
On a race. Ah! cautious man whom no sin depraves.

And it won't add up, at least in my mind,
To what it takes in the living poetry stakes.
I don't care what Chicago thinks; I am blind
To college lecturers and the breed of fakes:
I mean to say I'm not blind really,
I have my eyes wide open, as you may imagine,
And I am aware of our own boys, such as Ben Kiely,
Buying and selling literature on the margin.
Yes, Yeats, it was damn easy for you, protected
By the middle classes and the Big Houses,
To talk about the sixty-year-old public protected
Man sheltered by the dim Victorian Muses.

Notes

Address to an Old Wooden Gate

First publication and source text: *Dundalk Democrat* (2 February 1929).

The first poems Kavanagh published were those entered for a weekly poetry competition in the *Irish Weekly Independent* between September 1928 and June 1929 (he was occasionally a runner-up) and this one, printed in a local newspaper.

'scringes' is a colloquial word meaning 'rasping sounds'.

The Intangible

First publication: *Irish Statesman* (19 October 1929).

Source text: *Ploughman and Other Poems* (1936).

His first publication in a literary journal, this poem originally concluded with the couplet, 'Two and two do not make four / On every shore.'

Ploughman

First publication: *Irish Statesman* (15 February 1930).

Source text: *Ploughman and Other Poems* (1936).

This poem was included by Thomas Moult in *The Best Poems of 1930* (London, 1930).

To a Blackbird

First publication: *Spectator* (9 May 1931).

Source text: *Ploughman and Other Poems* (1936).

Kavanagh's first publication in a British journal.

Gold Watch

First publication: *Spectator* (20 June 1931).

Source text: *Ploughman and Other Poems* (1936).

Beech Tree

First publication: *Dublin Magazine* (October/December 1931) as 'The Beech Tree'.
    Source text: *Ploughman and Other Poems* (1936).

To a Child

First publication: *Dublin Magazine* (October/December 1931).
    Source text: *Ploughman and Other Poems* (1936).
    In *Self-Portrait* (1964) Kavanagh described this as the first poem in which he had become 'airborne'.

My Room

First publication and source text: *Dublin Magazine* (April/June 1933).

Four Birds

First publication: *Dublin Magazine* (April/June 1934) as 'Seven Birds'.
    Source text: *Ploughman and Other Poems* (1936).

To a Late Poplar

First publication: *John O'London's Weekly* (May 1934).
    Source text: *Ploughman and Other Poems* (1936).

After May

First publication: *Irish Times* (15 June 1935).
    Source text: *Ploughman and Other Poems* (1936).

Tinker's Wife

First publication and source text: *Ploughman and Other Poems* (1936).

April

First publication and source text: *Ploughman and Other Poems* (1936).

Inniskeen Road: July Evening

First publication and source text: *Ploughman and Other Poems* (1936).

March

First publication and source text: *Ploughman and Other Poems* (1936).

Sanctity

First publication: *Dublin Magazine* (July/September 1936).
  Source text: *A Soul for Sale* (1947).

Monaghan Hills

First publication and source text: *Dublin Magazine* (July/September 1936).

The Hired Boy

First publication and source text: *Ireland Today* (October 1936).
  The parish of Donaghmoyne is adjacent to Inniskeen.

My People

First publication and source text: *Dublin Magazine* (January/March 1937).

Shancoduff

First publication: *Dublin Magazine* (July/September 1937), as 'Shanco Dubh'.
Heavily revised for John Arlott (ed.), *First Time in America* (New York, 1948)
and *Nimbus* (winter, 1956).
  Source text: *Come Dance with Kitty Stobling and Other Poems* (1960).
  Title: Reynolds' Farm, a sixteen-acre farm purchased by Kavanagh's father,
was in the townland of Shancoduff.
  'Big Forth' is a prehistoric hill-fort; Kavanagh always used this spelling of
'fort'.
  Glassdrummond is in County Down.

April Dusk

First publication: *Complete Poems* (New York, 1972).
    Source text: *The Seed and the Soil* (1937), unpublished collection (MS 9579), National Library of Ireland.

Poplar Memory

First publication: *Complete Poems* (New York, 1972).
    Source text: *The Seed and the Soil* (1937).
    'From' in line 4 has been substituted for the MS 'For'.

Poet

First publication and source text: *Dublin Magazine* (January/March 1938).

Pursuit of an Ideal

First publication and source text: *Dublin Magazine* (January/March 1938).

In the Same Mood

First publication and source text: *Dublin Magazine* (January/March 1938).

The Irony of It

First publication and source text: *Irish Times* (14 February 1938).

Plough-horses

First publication and source text: *Fifty Years of Modern Verse*, ed. John Gawsworth (London, 1938).

Snail

First publication: *Complete Poems* (New York, 1972).
    Source text: *To Anna Quinn* (1938), unpublished collection (MS 9579), National Library of Ireland.

The Weary Horse

First publication: *Complete Poems* (New York, 1972).
Source text: *To Anna Quinn* (1938). Untitled.
Line 7: 'look' instead of 'book' in the ms. seems to be a slip of the pen.

Pygmalion

First publication: *Collected Poems* (1964).
Source text: *To Anna Quinn* (1938).
In MS 3215 in the National Library of Ireland line 12 reads 'Once lipped to grey terrific smile'.

Anna Quinn

First publication and source text: *Dublin Magazine* (October/December 1939).

Primrose

First publication: *Dublin Magazine* (October/December 1939).
Source text: *A Soul for Sale* (1947).

Memory of My Father

First publication: *Dublin Magazine* (October/December 1939).
Source text: *A Soul for Sale* (1947).
The poet's father, James Kavanagh, died on 27 August 1929.
Gardiner Street is in Dublin.

Christmas, 1939

First publication and source text: *Capuchin Annual* (Christmas 1939).

Christmas Eve Remembered

First publication and source text: *Irish Independent* (23 December 1939).

To the Man After the Harrow

First publication: *Irish Times* (6 April 1940).
Source text: *Come Dance with Kitty Stobling and Other Poems* (1960).

Spraying the Potatoes

First publication: *Irish Times* (27 July 1940).

Source text: *A Soul for Sale* (1947).

Title: Potato plants (of which Kerr's Pinks and Arran Banners are two varieties) were sprayed with chemicals to prevent disease or 'blight'. On small farms the farmer walked along each row of plants (drill) with a two-gallon sprayer strapped to his back, filling it from a large barrel. Copper sulphate was used, hence 'copper-poisoned'.

Pilgrims

Unpublished. Written in summer 1940.

Source text: Frank O'Connor papers, Mugar Memorial Library, Boston City University.

The three pilgrimages referred to are: the annual pilgrimage to Lady Well near Dundalk, described in *The Green Fool*, chapter 6; the climb to the top of Croagh Patrick mountain near Westport, County Mayo, which Kavanagh reported on for the *Irish Independent* newspaper in July 1940; Saint Patrick's Purgatory, Lough Derg (see note on *Lough Derg* below).

Stony Grey Soil

First publication: *The Bell* (October 1940).

Source text: *A Soul for Sale* (1947).

Published in the opening number of *The Bell*, the poem was dedicated to Sean O'Faolain, founding editor of the journal. It was paired with a more complimentary but much weaker poem apostrophizing a local townland, entitled 'Kednaminsha'. (Kavanagh had attended Kednaminsha school.)

Mullahinsha, Drummeril and Black Shanco (Shancoduff) are townlands in the parish of Inniskeen.

A Christmas Childhood

First publication: part I in the *Irish Press* (24 December 1943); part II in *The Bell* (December 1940).

Source text: *A Soul for Sale* (1947).

Art McCooey

First publication: *The Bell* (April 1941).

Source text: *A Soul for Sale* (1947).

Art McCooey (Mac Cumhaigh) was a popular Gaelic-speaking poet who lived in Creggan, County Armagh, quite near Inniskeen, and worked as a farm labourer. Kavanagh's knowledge of Gaelic was rudimentary, but he felt an affection for the Gaelic-speaking poets of his own region: '. . . though they were not great poets, they absorbed the little fields and lanes and became authentic through them' (*APC*, p. 28. See top of p. xxxiii).

'Wangel' is a dialect word for a handful of straw tied at one end.

The Long Garden

First publication: *Listener* (11 December 1941).

Source text: *A Soul for Sale* (1947).

See note on *Why Sorrow?* below.

Carrick is Carrickmacross, the nearest town to Inniskeen; Candlefort and Drumcatton are in the parish of Inniskeen.

Why Sorrow?

Source text: Undated typescript (Kav/B/40) in the Kavanagh Archive, University College Dublin.

Probably the first of the three long narrative poems composed between 1940 and 1942, although difficult to date precisely. Lines 97–124 were excerpted in 1941, revised into a first person plural narrative and published as 'The Long Garden' (above), but the poem's concluding sequence on Lough Derg may date from Kavanagh's first pilgrimage in June 1940 or his second in June 1942 (see *Lough Derg* below). Four pages are missing from the typescript between pages 9 and 14, and the ending is lost. 'Father Mat', which was quarried from it in 1945 (see below), may have incorporated some material from the missing pages. *Why Sorrow?* was submitted to the Cuala Press, which rejected it in January 1944.

Seola is a townland in the parish of Inniskeen.

The Great Hunger

First publication: parts I, II, III and twenty-six lines from part IV under the title 'The Old Peasant' in *Horizon*, vol. 5, no. 25 (January 1942), with a note that this 'is a long poem of 30 pages of which only the beginning is . . . given'.

The complete poem, with parts I, II, III revised and part IV substantially changed, was published by the Cuala Press, Dublin, in April 1942 in an expensive limited edition of 250 copies. A bowdlerized version, omitting ll. 9–32 of part II, but otherwise only slightly revised, was the concluding poem in *A Soul for Sale* (1947). When Kavanagh made a holograph copy of *The Great Hunger* for the National Library of Ireland, he inserted a note that the poem was completed in October 1941. *The Great Hunger* was out of print from 1947 until *Collected Poems* (1964).

Source text: *The Great Hunger*, Cuala Press (1942).

Title: Since Cecil Woodham-Smith's *The Great Hunger* (London, 1962; Penguin, Harmondsworth, 1991), a study of the great Irish famine of 1845–7, the phrase has become synonymous with this famine. It was not common currency before 1962 (I have been unable to find a single usage of it before that date as a synonym for the 1845–7 famine), and Kavanagh maintained that Woodham-Smith had stolen his title; nevertheless, the poem's recurrent imagery of potato harvesting does appear to allude to the great famine.

Censorship and bowdlerization: The edition of *Horizon* in which part of *The Great Hunger* first appeared was an 'Irish number' which was seized by the Irish police acting under the Emergency Powers legislation of 1939. They questioned the poet but took no further action in the matter. It was expected that the Cuala Press edition of the poem would be banned by the Censorship Board on grounds of indecency, but it escaped their notice, possibly because it had a very limited circulation. The police had leaned on the Irish distributors, Browne and Nolan, not to stock it, so copies had to be ordered directly from the publisher. The bowdlerization of all but the first stanza of part II in the *A Soul for Sale* edition was done at Kavanagh's suggestion because he thought the lines were 'perhaps too obscene'. He asked the London publisher of *Collected Poems* to return to the unexpurgated Cuala Press version of the poem.

I

'spanging' means striding; 'ruckety' means uneven; 'sole-plate' is part of a plough.

'a wet sack flapping about the knees': field workers sometimes wore a sack as an apron to protect their clothes.

'The horse lifts its head and cranes': 'crashes' for 'cranes' in the Cuala version is probably a misprint.

III

'whirring stone', revised from 'whirring noise' for *A Soul for Sale*.

'Hop back . . . wae': Maguire's instructions to his horse; 'Woa' means to slow down or stop.

All previous editions have 'prostitute's', which is clearly a misprint.

XI

Matt Talbot (1856–1925) was a Dublin docker who was an alcoholic until the age of twenty-eight, when he reformed and thereafter devoted his leisure time to prayer and penance. At his death it was discovered that he wore chains on his body. Talbot gave alms to the needy and was particularly friendly towards children; like Maguire, he lived with his mother until her death. A model for recovering alcoholics, he was given the title Venerable by the Church.

XII

'the tick'. The mattress. Ticking was the striped fabric in which a mattress was encased.

XIV

Lammas is 1 August.

'an oil-less lamp'. Oil lamps were still the norm in rural Ireland in 1942; electricity was not switched on in Inniskeen until 17 December 1953.

'No hope. No. No lust.' in Cuala Press version. The omission of the second 'No', as in *A Soul for Sale*, seems preferable.

Lough Derg

First publication: *November Haggard*, ed. Peter Kavanagh (New York, 1971).

Published in book form by Martin, Brian and O'Keeffe, London, and the Goldsmith Press, the Curragh (Ireland), in 1978.

Source text: Typescript (Kav/B/1) in the Kavanagh Archive, University College Dublin. The only surviving typescript version, this includes several variants on the 1971 and 1978 versions.

Kavanagh reported on the three-day pilgrimage for the *Irish Independent* newspaper in June 1940 (unpublished) and for the *Standard*, a Catholic weekly

(12 June 1942). The poem was written soon after the 1942 pilgrimage; the address on the typescript is '9, Lr. O'Connell St, Dublin', to which Kavanagh moved on 30 June 1942. It is likely that *Lough Derg* was included in the collection *A Satirical Pilgrimage*, rejected by the Cuala Press in 1944 and by Faber and Faber in 1945.

Title: Lough Derg is the name of the lake in County Donegal on which the island known as 'St Patrick's Purgatory' is situated. The island has been a place of pilgrimage since the Middle Ages, and making the pilgrimage is usually referred to as 'doing Lough Derg'.

'Congresses'. A eucharistic congress held in Dublin in June 1932 was attended by over a million Catholics.

Muckno Street is in the town of Castleblayney, County Monaghan.

'Prior'. The priest who oversees the pilgrimages.

'agnisties' is the plural of a colloquial pronunciation of the Latin phrase Agnus Dei (Lamb of God). The Agnus Dei was a small wax or silken padded disc, stamped with the device of a lamb bearing a cross or flag; blessed by the Church, it was treated as a devotional object by some pious Catholics.

'Catholic Truth pamphlets'. The Catholic Truth Society of Ireland, founded in 1899, attempted to counter the spread of immoral literature by publishing and distributing popular, inexpensive pamphlets and tracts.

AOH is the Ancient Order of Hibernians, a Catholic counter-organization to the Protestant Orange Order, founded in 1838 but politically active in the twentieth century.

Ireland 'froze for want of Europe' because its policy of neutrality during the Second World War isolated it from the rest of Europe.

'Intermediate'. The Intermediate Certificate was a public examination which pupils sat after two or three years in a secondary school. It has since been replaced.

'Dempsey . . . Tunney'. Jack Dempsey (1895–1983) was world heavyweight boxing champion from 1919 to 1926, when he lost his title to Gene Tunney (1897–1978). He lost to Tunney again in 1927 and this fight, known as 'the battle of the Long Count', was one of the most controversial in boxing history. Dempsey retired from the ring in 1940.

Cornelius Jansen (1585–1638) inspired the religious revival known as Jansenism, an attempt to reform the Church of Rome. In Ireland, Jansenism is particularly associated with sexual repression and Kavanagh subscribed to a widespread view that priests trained in Maynooth were infected by this 'anti-life heresy'.

Rostov, on the river Don in southern Russia, was under attack by Germany in June 1942 and was captured at the end of July.

Advent

First publication: *Irish Times* (24 December 1942) as 'Renewal'.

Source text: *A Soul for Sale* (1947), but there the first sonnet was divided into two stanzas.

Beyond the Headlines

First publication and source text: *Irish Press* (29 March 1943).

Consider the Grass Growing

First publication and source text: *Irish Press* (21 May 1943). Untitled.

Threshing Morning

First publication: A variant version of the first three stanzas, entitled 'A Reverie of Poor Piers', in Kavanagh's City Commentary column, *Irish Press* (27 September 1943). A variant version of the remainder of the poem, entitled 'Threshing Morning', is included in a holograph collection, *Poems*, c.1929–40, MS 3215 in the National Library of Ireland. (The page containing the first three stanzas has been removed, probably for use in the *Irish Press*.) The entire poem was first published in *Tarry Flynn* (1948, pp. 188–9) and this novel also includes a variant version of the fourth stanza (p. 91).

Source text: *Tarry Flynn* (London, 1948). Untitled. Title from MS 3215.

October, 1943

First publication and source text: *Irish Press* (27 October 1943).

Peace

Source text: *Come Dance with Kitty Stobling and Other Poems* (1960), where it is dated 1943.

A Wreath for Tom Moore's Statue

First publication: *Irish Times* (4 March 1944) as 'Statue, Symbol and Poet'.

Source text: *A Soul for Sale* (1947).

The poem alludes to the laying of a wreath on the poet's statue in College Street, Dublin, by six members of a newly formed Thomas Moore Society on 25 February 1944, the ninety-first anniversary of his death. The ceremony aroused little public interest: there were only about twenty spectators.

Moore's statue, which stands beside Trinity College Dublin, has been described by his biographer as 'a libel in metal, holding him up to posterity's ridicule and contempt' (Terence de Vere White, *Tom Moore*, London, 1977, p. xii).

Pegasus

First publication: *Irish Times* (1 July 1944) as 'A Glut on the Market'.

Source text: *A Soul for Sale* (1947), where it was the opening poem.

Kavanagh's *Irish Press* column was terminated in February 1944 and he had no regular employment until August 1945.

Memory of Brother Michael

First publication: *Irish Times* (14 October 1944).

Source text: *A Soul for Sale* (1947).

Title: Brother Michael (1575–*c*.1645), a Franciscan monk, was a historian who, between 1632 and 1636, compiled with the aid of three other historians *Annala Rioghachta Eireann* (Annals of the Kingdom of Ireland), commonly known as *The Annals of the Four Masters*. The *Annals* are mostly a chronicle of facts and dates, recording the history of Ireland to 1616. Brother Michael's historiography was important because it preserved information which might otherwise have been lost with the destruction of manuscripts and the suppression of the old Gaelic order after the Cromwellian plantations.

Brendan was a sixth-century Irish saint who was the hero of an eighth-century Latin prose masterpiece, *Navigatio Brendani* (The Voyage of St Brendan), a tale of adventures at sea which includes the saint's voyage to America.

This poem was a favourite with anthologists, but from the mid-1950s Kavanagh began refusing permission to republish it. He repudiated it both because it was 'bad history' and because of 'how appallingly' it accepted 'the myth of Ireland as a spiritual entity' (*Studies*, spring 1959).

Bluebells for Love

First publication: *The Bell* (June 1945) as 'Bluebells'.
Source text: *A Soul for Sale* (1947).
Line 1: 'big trees' was originally 'beech trees'.
The poem commemorates a visit to Lord Dunsany's castle in County Meath in the company of Hilda Moriarty, who is also the heroine of 'On Raglan Road' (see note below).

Temptation in Harvest

First publication: The first three sonnets, with some variants, were published in the *Irish Times* (1 September 1945) as 'The Monaghan Accent', with a note that this was 'a fragment from a sequence'. The final two sonnets, with some variants, appeared in the *Irish Times* (29 June 1946) under the present title; an accompanying note indicates that they are the end of a sequence.
Source text: *A Soul for Sale* (1947).
'Flaggers' are wild irises which grow on marshy ground.

Father Mat

First publication: The first two stanzas, untitled, in the *Standard* (5 October 1945); the last three stanzas of part II and all part III were printed as a continuous poem, entitled 'Through the Open Door . . .' in *Irish Writing*, no. 1 (October 1945), followed by a note: 'the above lines are taken from a poem Father Mat.'
See also note on *Why Sorrow?* (above).
Source text: *A Soul for Sale* (1947).

In Memory of My Mother

First publication: *Standard* (7 December 1945).
Source text: *Come Dance with Kitty Stobling and Other Poems* (1960).
The poet's mother, Bridget Kavanagh, died suddenly in her seventy-third year on 10 November 1945.

On Raglan Road

First publication: *Irish Press* (3 October 1946) as 'Dark-Haired Miriam Ran Away'.

Source text: *Poems* (1955). Unpublished collection. Line 7 was originally: 'Synthetic sighs and fish-dim eyes and all death's loud display'.

The poet lived in a boarding house at 19 Raglan Road between autumn 1944 and October 1945. The poem, which records his unrequited romance with Hilda Moriarty, a medical student (see 'Bluebells for Love', above), is set to the air 'The Dawning of the Day'. Popularized by the singer Luke Kelly of the Dubliners in the mid-1960s, it has become one of Kavanagh's best-known lyrics.

Jim Larkin

First publication and source text: *The Bell* (March 1947).

An elegy for the labour leader James Larkin, who had died on 30 January. Larkin founded the Irish Transport and General Workers' Union (ITGWU) in 1908. The employers' attempt to prevent their workers from joining this union resulted in a lock-out in September 1913; 25,000 men remained unemployed until the following January/February.

The Wake of the Books

First publication and source text: *The Bell* (November 1947).

This sketch was a response to the editor Peadar O'Donnell's suggestion in the July 1947 issue that a ceremonial wake be held annually to mourn the year's censored books. Censorship of books in Ireland, introduced in 1929, was widely regarded as draconian by writers and intellectuals, because many international classics, as well as Irish-authored books, were banned; Kavanagh's attitude, as illustrated in the Prologue, was unusual. When *Tarry Flynn* was banned a year later, he welcomed the notoriety: 'Good advert' was how he put it. The novel was swiftly unbanned by an Appeals Board set up in 1946 to review individual cases.

'sauntered by the Lee'. Sean O'Faolain (1900–1991) and Frank O'Connor (1903–66) both hailed from Cork (situated on the river Lee). Both were vociferous opponents of censorship. The banned books listed are O'Faolain's collection *Midsummer Night Madness and other stories* (1932); Kathleen Winsor's best-selling bodice-ripper *Forever Amber* (1944), Kate O'Brien's *The Land of Spices* (1941), banned because of a decorous allusion to homosexuality in one sentence, and *The Midnight Court* (1945), Frank O'Connor's English translation of Brian Merriman's eighteenth-century Irish-language master-piece, *Cúirt an Mheán-Oíche*, which deals with the topic of sexual repression in Catholic Ireland.

The RDS (Royal Dublin Society) lending library in Ballsbridge would have had a more upmarket clientele than the Carnegie or public libraries.

Alfred O'Rahilly (1884–1969), a professor and Registrar at University College Cork, was also a member of the banking commission and author of a large tome entitled *Money* (1942).

Reggie (Reginald) Segrave-Daly owned apple-orchards near Gowran in County Kilkenny; he was in the habit of writing to the *Irish Times* on apple-related matters in the 1940s.

Frank O'Connor had moved his family to London for the first half of 1947.

The Editor is Bertie Smyllie of the *Irish Times*; this newspaper had openly supported Britain in the 1939–45 war. Despite paper rationing, it maintained a Saturday Literary Page where some of Kavanagh's own poems were first published. *Gradh* is the Irish word for love.

Austin Clarke (1896–1974), a poet, novelist and critic whose literary views Kavanagh abhorred because Clarke wanted Irish poetry in English to imitate the techniques of Irish-language verse.

The fight around the bier of censored books recalls the notorious fight in the Palace Bar in 1941 when its literary habitués, who included Austin Clarke and M. J. MacManus (1888–1951), the literary editor of the *Irish Press*, came to blows over Louis MacNeice. Kavanagh, who was present, wrote an account of the 'wild hooey over Louis' in 'The Ballad of the Palace Bar', most of which is now lost. The second MacManus referred to is the novelist Francis MacManus (1909–65).

The Scuttery is a pseudonym for the Buttery, a fashionable bar in the Royal Hibernian Hotel.

Captain Boycott (1946), a novel by Philip Rooney (1907–62).

Colum is Padraic Colum (1881–1972), poet and Abbey dramatist, who had emigrated to the United States in 1914.

Cumann – the Fianna Fáil political party, then in government, was organized at local level into branches known by the Irish name Cumann.

Ná habair é is an Irish phrase meaning 'Don't mention it'.

The four stanzas beginning 'Sometimes I can see in these poor streets' were published as a separate poem, 'October, Dublin', in John Arlott (ed.), *First Time in America* (New York, 1948).

Jungle

First publication: *Irish Times* (25 September 1948).

Source text: *Poems* (1955). Unpublished collection.

Kavanagh rented an apartment at 62 Pembroke Road from September 1943 to October 1958; Clyde Road and Waterloo Road are nearby.

No Social Conscience

First publication: *Irish Times* (15 January 1949) as 'The Hero'.

Source text: *Poems* (1955).

The Paddiad

First publication: *Horizon* (August 1949).

Source text: *Come Dance with Kitty Stobling and Other Poems* (1960) where it is prefaced by this 'Note':

> This satire is based on the sad notion with which my youth was infected that Ireland was a spiritual entity. I had a good deal to do with putting an end to this foolishness, for as soon as I found out I reported the news widely. It is now only propagated by the BBC in England and in the Bronx in New York and the Departments of Irish literature at Princeton, Yale, Harvard and New York universities.
>
> I have included this satire but wish to warn the reader that it is based on the above-mentioned false and ridiculous premises.

Kavanagh privately identified the Paddies: 'Paddy of the Celtic Mist – Austin Clarke and other personalities; Chestertonian Paddy Frog – Robert Farren; in their middle sits a fellow – Maurice Walsh and other personalities' (Kav/B/80, Kavanagh Archive, University College Dublin).

Austin Clarke. See 'The Wake of the Books' (above). Robert Farren (1909–84), who preferred to style himself Roibeard Ó Faracháin, was a poet, critic and Talks Officer, later Controller of Programmes, for Radio Éireann. He was a friend of Austin Clarke, and Kavanagh's hostility to both writers was largely based on their promotion of an ethnic aesthetic. Kavanagh's review of Farren's book about poetry in Ireland, *The Course of Irish Verse* (1947), was so abusive that the *Irish Times* refused to print it.

Maurice Walsh (1879–1964) was a best-selling novelist from Kerry.

Mediocrity was one of Kavanagh's favourite terms of abuse.

The volume of Sean O'Casey's autobiography entitled *Inishfallen, Fare Thee Well* was published in 1949.

Spring Day

First publication: *Envoy* (March 1950). Untitled.

Source text: *Poems* (1955).

Commenting on this poem, which draws on the 'Come all ye' type of Irish ballad, Kavanagh acknowledged that it was 'not a complete success' but that the ballad genre could prove useful to poets: 'There is health in the barbaric simplicity of the ballad; it compels one to say something. Most of the verse written in this land suffers from one thing – it has nothing to say. Having something to say is largely a mood' (*Envoy*, March 1950).

Leave Them Alone

First publication: *Envoy* (May 1950). Untitled.

Source text: *Poems* (1955).

Adventure in the Bohemian Jungle

First publication: *Envoy* (July 1950) as 'A Play'.

Source text: *Poems* (1955).

'A ball' is 'A ball of malt', meaning 'a glass of whiskey'.

'CCL' stands for Catholic Cultural League.

'McCormick, Ireland's soul' refers to the highly talented comic actor F. J. McCormick.

'gurriers' are Dublin working-class louts.

Ante-natal Dream

First publication: *Envoy* (July 1950).

Source text: *Come Dance with Kitty Stobling and Other Poems* (1960).

Bank Holiday

First publication: *Envoy* (September 1950) as 'Testament'.

Source text: *Poems* (1955).

The Waterloo and Searson's on Upper Baggot Street were the two pubs closest to Kavanagh's apartment on Pembroke Road.

Irish Poets Open Your Eyes

First publication and source text: *Envoy* (September 1950). Untitled.

In Kavanagh's *Envoy* 'Diary' this poem is prefaced by the comment: 'A new version of Yeats's poem ['Under Ben Bulben'] is called for.'

There is a greyhound race-track at Shelbourne Park in Dublin.

Tale of Two Cities

First publication: *Envoy* (October 1950). Untitled.

Source text: *Poems* (1955).

Harry Kelly, Jack Sullivan and Brady were 'Harry Kernoff and Seumas O'Sullivan and Smyllie' in *Envoy*, and Galligan was Oliver St John Gogarty.

To Be Dead

First publication: *Envoy* (October 1950). Untitled.

Source text: *Come Dance with Kitty Stobling and Other Poems* (1960).

Kerr's Ass

First publication: *Envoy* (October 1950). Untitled. Republished under the present title in *The Bell* (September 1953).

Source text: *Come Dance with Kitty Stobling and Other Poems* (1960).

The poem was first quoted in Kavanagh's *Envoy* 'Diary', where he argued that the speed of modern air travel had rendered the term 'exile' melodramatic.

The Defeated

First publication and source text: *Envoy* (February 1951) as 'A Sonnet Sequence for the Defeated'.

Source text: *Poems* (1955).

Padraic Colum. See 'The Wake of the Books', above.

Who Killed James Joyce?

First publication and source text: *Envoy* (April 1951), a special Joyce number of *Envoy* commemorating the tenth anniversary of his death.

Despite this ironic commentary on the burgeoning Joyce cult in academe, Kavanagh was himself a great admirer of Joyce's writings.

'Surely not Bertie' alludes to William Robert (Bertie) Rodgers (1909–69), poet and broadcaster. A Presbyterian minister at Loughgall, County Antrim, he resigned his ministry to take up a post with the BBC Third Programme in London. He presented a series of broadcasts on Irish writers, including one on Joyce, later collected in *Irish Literary Portraits* (London, 1972). All Saints' Church at Langham Place, London, is close to Broadcasting House.

Though the Joyce cult is mocked in the poem, Kavanagh himself made the Bloomsday pilgrimage on 16 June 1954 with John Ryan, editor of *Envoy*, and fellow-writers Brian O'Nolan (better known as Flann O'Brien) and Anthony Cronin.

'Martello Tower to the cabby's shelter'. The Bloomsday pilgrimage begins at the Martello tower in Sandycove, where the opening sequence in *Ulysses* is set; the penultimate stop is at the site of the Eumaeus episode, the cabman's shelter under the Loop Line bridge, just west of the Custom House.

Portrait of the Artist

First publication: *Envoy* (May 1951). Untitled.

Source text: *Nimbus* (winter 1956).

This issue of *Nimbus* included a mini-collection of Kavanagh's previously uncollected poetry, nineteen poems in all, with an accompanying essay by Anthony Cronin, 'Innocence and Experience: The Poetry of Patrick Kavanagh'.

Auditors In

First publication: *The Bell* (October 1951), where it was subtitled 'Speculations on a Theme'.

Source text: *Come Dance with Kitty Stobling and Other Poems* (1960).

Ednamo is a townland in the parish of Inniskeen; Willie Hughes's house actually existed.

In the first sonnet in part II, line 10 begins with 'Or' in the source text, a misprint.

Innocence

First publication and source text: *The Bell* (November 1951).

'Big Forth'. See note on 'Shancoduff', above.

Epic

First publication: *The Bell* (November 1951).
  Source text: *Come Dance with Kitty Stobling and Other Poems* (1960).
  A 'march' is a boundary.
  Ballyrush and Gortin are townlands in the parish of Inniskeen.

On Looking into E. V. Rieu's Homer

First publication: *The Bell* (November 1951).
  Source text: *Come Dance with Kitty Stobling and Other Poems* (1960).
  E. V. Rieu's translation of Homer's *Iliad* was first published in 1950.

God in Woman

First publication and source text: *The Bell* (November 1951).

I Had a Future

First publication and source text: *Kavanagh's Weekly* (12 April 1952).
  On first taking up residence in Dublin in August 1939, Kavanagh lived in a bedsitter at 51 Upper Drumcondra Road.
  The poet John Betjeman, who was press attaché to the UK Representative to Éire from January 1941 to August 1943, befriended Kavanagh.

Wet Evening in April

First publication and source text: *Kavanagh's Weekly* (19 April 1952).

The Ghost Land

First publication and source text: *Kavanagh's Weekly* (26 April 1952), under the pen-name J. P. McCabe.

The Road to Hate

First publication and source text: *Kavanagh's Weekly* (3 May 1952), under the pen-name Laurence Pepper.

The God of Poetry

First publication and source text: *Kavanagh's Weekly* (24 May 1952), under the pen-name Ann McKenna.

A Ballad

First publication and source text: *Kavanagh's Weekly* (14 June 1952), under the initials K.H.

Having Confessed

First publication: *Kavanagh's Weekly* (5 July 1952). Untitled.
  Source text: *Poems* (1955).
  The final issue of *Kavanagh's Weekly* concluded with this poem.

If Ever You Go to Dublin Town

First publication: *Irish Times* (21 March 1953).
  Source text: *Come Dance with Kitty Stobling and Other Poems* (1960).

The Rowley Mile

First publication and source text: *The Bell* (January 1954).
  This and the following poem were published together as 'Two Sentimental Songs'.

Cyrano de Bergerac

First publication and source text: *The Bell* (January 1954).
  Reviewing a film based on Edmond Rostand's play *Cyrano de Bergerac*, Kavanagh commented that Cyrano's disability was 'a symbol of the price by which every gift is bought' (*Kavanagh's Weekly*, 21 June 1952).

The Hero

First publication: *The Bell* (March 1954) as 'Dublin'.
  Source text: *Nimbus* (winter 1956).

Intimate Parnassus

First publication: *The Bell* (March 1954).
  Source text: *Come Dance with Kitty Stobling and Other Poems* (1960).

On Reading a Book on Common Wild Flowers

First publication and source text: *The Bell* (March 1954).

Narcissus and the Women

First publication and source text: *The Bell* (March 1954).

Irish Stew

First publication and source text: *The Bell* (March 1954).
  The Irish politician satirized in this monologue is probably Frank Aiken of Fianna Fáil, who as Minister for External Affairs had intervened in 1951 to veto the Cultural Relations Committee's recommendation that Kavanagh's fare and expenses be paid to give readings in the USA; shortly afterwards, when the Committee proposed sending Kavanagh as a delegate to a conference in Brussels, Aiken directed that Austin Clarke or Roibeard Ó Faracháin be sent instead.

The Christmas Mummers

First publication and source text: *Nimbus* (winter 1954), where the poem was accompanied by the following 'Explanations':

> The custom of Mummers or rhymers going around before Christmas performing in rural kitchens still lives on in some parts of Ireland. Each Mummer represents some historical or nonsensical character. The formula is exactly as in this piece.
>
> The Hitler war was known officially in Southern Ireland as 'The Emergency'.
>
> Owen Roe. Owen Roe O'Sullivan was in the front rank of the ten thousand Irish poets of his day. The standing army of Irish poets seldom falls below this figure.
>
> Football prowess in Ireland, as in Hungary today, has always been a path to political success.

Contrived, manufactured verse with its necessary lack of any passionate impulse or belief is what passed for poetry among the Gaels. Phrase-making. The poet was a romantically wild man who was seldom sober, was a devil for the women. Dylan Thomas brought this bogusity to the English who thought it new and wonderful.

New Statesmanism. *The New Statesman* is the name of an English radical weekly.

Mountjoy is the principal Dublin jail.

Working on the turf bogs in Ireland is equivalent to salt-mining in Siberia.

The surplus Irish population who cannot get into the BBC work in Birmingham where they are to be seen high up in the sky painting gasometers.

Prelude

First publication: *Irish Times* (12 February 1955) as 'From a Prelude'.
 Source text: *Come Dance with Kitty Stobling and Other Poems* (1960).

One Wet Summer

First publication: *Collected Poems* (1964).
 Source text: *Poems* (1955).

After Forty Years of Age

First publication: *Collected Poems* (1964).
 Source text: *Poems* (1955).

An Insult

First publication: *New Statesman* (21 February 1964).
 Source text: *Poems* (1955).

Nineteen Fifty-Four

First publication: *Nimbus* (summer 1956). Untitled.
 Source text: *Come Dance with Kitty Stobling and Other Poems* (1960).
 Nineteen fifty-four was an *annus horribilis* for Kavanagh. See Introduction, p. xxviii.

House Party to Celebrate the Destruction of the Roman Catholic Church in Ireland

First publication: *Nimbus* (winter 1956).

Source text: *Come Dance with Kitty Stobling and Other Poems* (1960).

The poem was written in response to a failed libel action which the parish priest of Doneraile in County Cork took as a result of Honor Tracy's satiric book about Ireland, *Mind You I've Said Nothing* (1953). The book had also satirized Kavanagh without naming him. Seamus represents Sean O'Faolain, who had an affair with Tracy.

The Hospital

First publication: *Nimbus* (winter 1956).

Source text: *Come Dance with Kitty Stobling and Other Poems* (1960).

Kavanagh was a patient in Ward 4 of the Rialto Hospital, Dublin, in March and April 1955; he was operated on for lung cancer on 31 March.

Leaves of Grass

First publication and source text: *Time and Tide* (1 December 1956).

October

First publication: *Encounter* (January 1958).

Source text: *Come Dance with Kitty Stobling and Other Poems* (1960).

Birth

First publication and source text: *Studies* (spring 1958).

Title: Kavanagh claimed that he had been born or reborn as a poet on the bank of Dublin's Grand Canal between the Baggot Street and Leeson Street bridges in July 1955. It was a warm summer and he was convalescing out of doors following his operation for lung cancer (see note on 'The Hospital' above).

Requiem for a Mill

First publication: *Studies* (spring 1958).
  Source text: *Come Dance with Kitty Stobling and Other Poems* (1960).
  Title: The poem was prompted by the closing-down of Carolan's corn-mill in Inniskeen.

Question to Life

First publication: *Time and Tide* (12 April 1958).
  Source text: *Come Dance with Kitty Stobling and Other Poems* (1960).

Come Dance with Kitty Stobling

First publication: *Encounter* (May 1958), as 'High Journey'.
  Source text: *Come Dance with Kitty Stobling and Other Poems* (1960).
  Title: Kitty Stobling is an invented name for the poet's muse.
  'colourful country': on its second journal publication in *Nonplus* (October 1959), the poem closed a sequence of poetry and prose which included 'three coloured sonnets' (see note on 'Yellow Vestment' below).

Is

First publication: *Encounter* (May 1958).
  Source text: *Come Dance with Kitty Stobling and Other Poems* (1960).

To Hell with Commonsense

First publication: *Encounter* (May 1958).
  Source text: *Come Dance with Kitty Stobling and Other Poems* (1960).

Canal Bank Walk

First publication: *Encounter* (May 1958).
  Source text: *Come Dance with Kitty Stobling and Other Poems* (1960).

Dear Folks

First publication: *Irish Times* (12 July 1958).
  Source text: *Come Dance with Kitty Stobling and Other Poems* (1960).

Song at Fifty

First publication: *Recent Poems* (1958). Limited edition.
First journal publication: *The Times Literary Supplement* (19 December 1958).
Source text: *Come Dance with Kitty Stobling and Other Poems* (1960).

Freedom

First publication: *Recent Poems* (1958).
First journal publication: *Nonplus* (October 1959).
Source text: *Come Dance with Kitty Stobling and Other Poems* (1960).

Lines Written on a Seat on the Grand Canal, Dublin

First publication: *Recent Poems* (1958).
First journal publication: *Studies* (spring 1959).
Source text: *Come Dance with Kitty Stobling and Other Poems* (1960).
Dermod O'Brien (1865–1945), a portrait, landscape and figure painter, was president of the Royal Hibernian Academy. He and his wife lived at 65 Fitzwilliam Square, near the Grand Canal.
A bench in Kavanagh's memory, erected on the bank of the Grand Canal at the fourth lock near Mespil Road, was unveiled on St Patrick's Day 1968. A bronze sculpture, by John Coll, of Kavanagh sitting on a bench, erected nearby, was unveiled on 11 June 1991.

The Self-slaved

First publication: *Recent Poems* (1958).
First journal publication: *Studies* (spring 1959).
Source text: *Come Dance with Kitty Stobling and Other Poems* (1960).

The One

First publication: *Recent Poems* (1958).
First journal publication: *Nonplus* (October 1959). Untitled.
Source text: *Come Dance with Kitty Stobling and Other Poems* (1960).

Yellow Vestment

First publication: *Recent Poems* (1958).
  First journal publication: *Nonplus* (October 1959). Untitled.
  Source text: *Come Dance with Kitty Stobling and Other Poems* (1960).
In *Nonplus* this sonnet was the first of a sequence of three which were numbered and described as 'three coloured sonnets'; the other two were 'Miss Universe' and 'The One'.

Love in a Meadow

First publication: *Recent Poems* (1958).
  First journal publication: *Nonplus* (October 1959). Untitled.
  Source text: *Come Dance with Kitty Stobling and Other Poems* (1960).
Toprass, an Inniskeen place-name, may have been chosen because it suggests high ground; Kavanagh was actually born in Mucker, which means 'place of pigs'.

Miss Universe

First publication: *Recent Poems* (1958).
  First journal publication: *Nonplus* (October 1959). Untitled.
  Source text: *Come Dance with Kitty Stobling and Other Poems* (1960).

Winter

First publication: *Nonplus* (October 1959).
  Source text: *Come Dance with Kitty Stobling and Other Poems* (1960).

Living in the Country

First publication and source text: *X*, vol. 1, no. 1 (November 1959).
This was the first number of *X*, a London-based avant-garde journal of literature and art, edited by the poet David Wright and the painter Patrick Swift, both close friends of Kavanagh's.
In *Collected Poems* (1964) this poem was presented as the first part of a two-part poem: the *X* text was 'Living in the Country: I' and 'The Poet's Ready Reckoner' (see note below) was 'Living in the Country: II'.

Lecture Hall

First publication and source text: *X*, vol. 1, no. 1 (November 1959).

News Item

First publication and source text: *Observer* (20 November 1960).

A covert love poem to Kavanagh's future wife, Katherine Barry Moloney; the poet often stayed with her in her apartment at 47 Gibson Square, in 1960 and 1961.

Paul Potts (1911–90) was a poet, critic and admirer of Kavanagh's poetry who lived in Islington.

Mermaid Tavern

First publication and source text: *X* (July 1962).

Literary Adventures

First publication and source text: *Poetry Ireland* (autumn 1962).

John Jordan (1930–88), a Dublin poet, short-story writer and academic, was a close friend of Kavanagh's. He edited this, the first number of the relaunched *Poetry Ireland*, while he was a TB patient in Dublin's Blanchardstown hospital.

John Lennon was an Inniskeen neighbour.

Sensational Disclosures!

First publication and source text: *Poetry Ireland* (spring 1963).

The Same Again

First publication and source text: *Arena* (spring 1963).

This was the first number of a Dublin-based avant-garde literary journal edited by James Liddy and Liam O'Connor and from the second number by Michael Hartnett. The young poet James Liddy was a fan of Kavanagh.

Thank You, Thank You

First publication and source text: *Arena* (spring 1963).

Kavanagh gave a spring series of extra-mural lectures at University College Dublin for several years, beginning in 1956.

About Reason, Maybe

First publication and source text: *Arena* (spring 1963).

That Garage

First publication and source text: *Arena* (spring 1963).

In Blinking Blankness: Three Efforts

First publication and source text: *Arena* (spring 1963).

Walter Lowenfels (1897–1976) published some poems in the *Irish Statesman*, the first literary and cultural journal Kavanagh ever read.

'the wren got caught in the furze': it was a St Stephen's Day (Boxing Day) custom in parts of rural Ireland for groups of youths, known as wren-boys, to call at neighbours' houses collecting money. Originally, they would have carried a dead wren. The verse or verses they recited varied from place to place; the Inniskeen version was:

> The wren, the wren, the king of all birds,
> On St Stephen's Day he got caught in the furze,
> Although he was little, his fame it was great,
> So get up Mrs —, and give us a treat.

The Poet's Ready Reckoner

First publication and source text: *Arena* (autumn 1963).

Kavanagh, who detested Brendan Behan, asked that 'Behaned' be printed in lower case when the poem was published in *Collected Poems* (1964) as 'Living in the Country: II'.

'My love . . . wreck of day': these lines echo the opening lines of Lord de Tablay's poem 'The Churchyard in the Sands': 'My love lies in the gates of foam / The last dear wreck of shore'.

A Summer Morning Walk

First publication and source text: *Arena* (summer 1964), where it was published as an excerpt from 'The Country' and dated 1962.

Personal Problem

First publication and source text: *Arena* (spring 1965).

Yeats

First publication and source text: *The Holy Door* (spring 1966).

The Holy Door was a new Dublin-based journal edited by the young poet Brian Lynch, fronting for James Liddy (see notes to 'The Same Again' above). This, the last poem Kavanagh published, was written in the wake of a Yeats centenary symposium in Northwestern University, Chicago, in April 1965, at which he was a guest speaker. His contribution provoked such outrage that the symposium broke up in disarray.

Appendix A: Author's Note to Collected Poems (1964)

I have never been much considered by the English critics. I suppose I shouldn't say this. But for many years I have learned not to care, and I have also learned that the basis of literary criticism is usually the ephemeral. To postulate even semi-absolute standards is to silence many lively literary men.

I would not object if some critic said I wasn't a poet at all. Indeed, trying to think of oneself as a poet is a peculiar business. What does it feel like to be a poet?

I am always shy of calling myself a poet and I wonder much at those young men and sometimes those old men who boldly declare their poeticality. If you ask them what they are, they say: Poet.

There is, of course, a poetic movement which sees poetry materialistically. The writers of this school see no transcendent nature in the poet: they are practical chaps, excellent technicians. But somehow or other I have a belief in poetry as a mystical thing, and a dangerous thing.

A man (I am thinking of myself) innocently dabbles in words and rhymes and finds that it is his life. Versing activity leads him away from the paths of conventional unhappiness. For reasons that I have never been able to explain, the making of verses has changed the course of one man's destiny. I could have been as happily unhappy as the ordinary countryman in Ireland. I might have stayed at the same moral age all my life. Instead of that, poetry made me a sort of outcast. And I was abnormally normal.

I do not believe in sacrifice and yet it seems I was sacrificed. I must avoid getting too serious.

I belong to neither of the two kinds of poet commonly known. There is the young chap who goes to school and university, is told by lecturers of the value of poetry, and there is the other kind whom we somehow think inspired. Lisping in numbers like Dylan Thomas, Burns, etc.

Looking back, I see that the big tragedy for the poet is poverty. I had no money and no profession except that of small farmer. And I had the misfortune to live the worst years of my life through a period when there were no Arts Councils, Foundations, Fellowships for the benefit of young poets.

On many occasions I literally starved in Dublin. I often borrowed a 'shilling for the gas' when in fact I wanted the coin to buy a chop. During the war, in Dublin, I did a column of gossip for a newspaper at four guineas a week.

I suppose when I come to think of it, if I had a stronger character, I might have done well enough for myself. But there was some kink in me, put there by Verse.

In 1942 I wrote *The Great Hunger*. Shortly after it was published a couple of hefty lads came to my lonely shieling on Pembroke Road. One of them had a copy of the poem behind his back. He brought it to the front and he asked me, 'Did you write that?' He was a policeman. It may seem shocking to the devotee of liberalism if I say that the police were right. For a poet in his true detachment is impervious to policemen. There is something wrong with a work of art, some kinetic vulgarity in it when it is visible to policemen.

The Great Hunger is concerned with the woes of the poor. A true poet is selfish and implacable. A poet merely states the position and does not care whether his words change anything or not. *The Great Hunger* is tragedy and Tragedy is underdeveloped Comedy, not fully born. Had I stuck to the tragic thing in *The Great Hunger* I would have found many powerful friends.

But I lost my messianic compulsion. I sat on the bank of the Grand Canal in the summer of 1955 and let the water lap idly on the shores of my mind. My purpose in life was to have no purpose.

Besides *The Great Hunger* there are many poems in this collection which I dislike; but I was too indifferent, too lazy to eliminate, change or collect. For these and other reasons I must offer thanks to Mr Martin Green who made the collection.*

* It was actually John Montague who made the collection, but this fact was kept secret from Kavanagh, who would probably have objected to another Irish poet editing his poetry. Martin Green was employed by the publishers, MacGibbon & Kee, and acted as go-between in some of their negotiations with Kavanagh.

Appendix B: Contents of Collections Published during Kavanagh's Lifetime

Ploughman and Other Poems, *Macmillan, London, 1936*

Ploughman; To a Blackbird; Mary; I May Reap; The Goat of Slieve Donard; Ascetic; The Intangible; Beech Tree; Soft Ease; A Star; Dark Ireland; To a Child; To a Late Poplar; Dreamer; Gold Watch; Twisted Furrows; Worship; Phoenix; After May; The Chase; Four Birds; Blind Dog; Tinker's Wife; April; To a Child; Inniskeen Road: July Evening; Pioneers; A Wind; At Noon; March; Morning.

A Soul for Sale, *Macmillan, London, 1947*

Pegasus; Father Mat; Temptation in Harvest; Bluebells for Love; Advent; A Christmas Childhood; Memory of My Father; The Long Garden; Primrose; Art McCooey; Spraying the Potatoes; Ethical; Sanctity; Candida; War and Peace; Stony Grey Soil; Memory of Brother Michael; A Wreath for Tom Moore's Statue; The Great Hunger.

Recent Poems, *Peter Kavanagh Hand Press, New York, 1958* (25 copies)

To Hell with Commonsense; Is; Canal Bank; October; Requiem for a Mill; Auditors In; Song at Fifty; Freedom; Dear Folks; Lines Written on a Seat on the Grand Canal, Dublin; The Self-slaved; The One; Yellow Vestment; Love in a Meadow; High Journey [Come Dance with Kitty Stobling]; Miss Universe; Prelude; If Ever You Go to Dublin Town; In Memory of My Mother; Epic.

Come Dance with Kitty Stobling and Other Poems, *Longmans, Green and Co., London, 1960 and Dufour Publications, Pennsylvania, 1960*

Canal Bank Walk; Lines Written on a Seat on the Grand Canal, Dublin; Is; To Hell with Commonsense; Requiem for a Mill; Auditors In; Song at Fifty; Dear Folks; Freedom; October; The Self-slaved; The One; Yellow Vestment; Love in a Meadow; Come Dance with Kitty Stobling; Miss Universe; Prelude; If Ever You Go to Dublin Town; In Memory of My Mother; Epic; Winter; Question to Life; To the Man After the Harrow; On Looking into E. V. Rieu's Homer; Kerr's Ass; Intimate Parnassus; Ante-natal Dream; To Be Dead; Peace; Shanco-duff; Nineteen Fifty-Four; The Hospital; The Hero; House Party; The Paddiad.

Collected Poems, *MacGibbon and Kee Ltd, London, 1964 and Devin-Adair, New York, 1964*

All poems in the three London-published collections and Plough-horses; From Tarry Flynn [Threshing Morning]; My Room; Pygmalion; Beyond the Headlines; Pursuit of an Ideal; In the Same Mood; The Road to Hate; Jungle; The Defeated; Bank Holiday; Adventures [sic] in the Bohemian Jungle; Irish Stew; The Christmas Mummers; Tale of Two Cities; Spring Day; Who Killed James Joyce?; Joyce's Ulysses; Portrait of the Artist; Leave Them Alone; Innocence; Cyrano de Bergerac; On Reading a Book on Common Wild Flowers; I Had a Future; The Rowley Mile; Wet Evening in April; Narcissus and the Women; God in Woman; After Forty Years of Age; Having Confessed; Lecture Hall; Living in the Country: I; Living in the Country: II [The Poet's Ready Reckoner]; Mermaid Tavern; One Wet Summer; The Gambler: A Ballet with Words; The Gambler: A Ballet; News Item; A Summer Morning Walk; A Ballad; No Social Conscience; An Insult; On Raglan Road; Literary Adventures; Sensational Disclosures! (Kavanagh Tells All); The Same Again; Thank You, Thank You; About Reason, Maybe; That Garage; In Blinking Blankness: Three Efforts.

Index of Titles

Index of First Lines